INTERNATIONAL CRITICAL
CRITICISM

PETER ABELARD

LEIF GRANE

Peter Abelard

Philosophy and Christianity in the Middle Ages

Translated by
FREDERICK AND CHRISTINE CROWLEY

Bibliography and Notes edited by
DEREK BAKER
M.A., B.Litt.
Lecturer in History, Edinburgh University

The King's Library

HARCOURT, BRACE & WORLD, INC.
NEW YORK

CONTENTS

CONTENTS

CHAPTER 1

The Twelfth Century Renaissance

Reassessment of the Middle Ages in European historiography commenced some centuries ago, but the traditional image of the Middle Ages as an intellectually dark period contributing nothing significant to human 'progress' has proved surprisingly durable. The period has generally been evaluated against the background of the concept of a classical renaissance, as developed in the nineteenth century – largely by *Jacob Burckhardt*. With the rebirth of the learning of Antiquity in the fifteenth and sixteenth centuries, all that had been left abandoned at the end of ancient times was revived. The term 'Middle Ages' came to signify a thousand-year lethargy characterized by the supremacy of the Church. Historians of philosophy showed an interest in the Greek philosophy of Antiquity, skipped the Middle Ages and continued with the Renaissance philosophers. What happened in the intervening period was of no particular interest. To be fair, it should be added that philosophers active around 1900 had grown up in a period during which mediaeval thought had in most quarters been treated with contempt, even from a theological viewpoint. This applied not only to Protestant research but equally to Catholic research. Most of our knowledge of mediaeval scientific scholasticism was not acquired until the present century. Pope Leo XIII was very active in encouraging the study of scholasticism, and on the Protestant side research into the Reformation, which was strongly challenged by this renewed interest in the Middle Ages, provided the inspiration. It was at first a matter of understanding and interpreting the existing printed material, but extensive research into manuscripts soon began. This made necessary a thorough reappraisal, not only of the relationship of mediaeval thought in general to Antiquity and Renaissance, but also of the area and extent of this thought.

It is not intended here to follow the course of this research, however exciting that might be. It is however indisputable that Burckhardt's conception of the Middle Ages has proved to be quite untenable, and any historical review of the concept of the Classical Renaissance with its associated concept of the 'Middle Ages' raises misgivings right from the outset. It is an absolute condition of historical research that matters should *be associated, one with another,* and that events and progress should be seen to be *conditioned* by what came before, by their 'causes'. This is a term from which most present-day historians would probably recoil, but this is no reason for us to stop looking at events *in connection with one another.* How otherwise could we *understand* whatever stands entirely alone? We understand by employing comparison and, faced with the *completely* exceptional, we are helpless. The classical concept of the Renaissance, which puts the Middle Ages in parentheses, in fact places us in this very situation. The concept is strangely abstract; it detaches the events of the Renaissance from their connection with what went before, and thus disregards that very understanding of 'the historical' which – quite apart from its truth – is the prerequisite of what we mean by historical research.

The doubts we may entertain, on grounds of principle alone, concerning this traditional concept have now been confirmed by the work on the Middle Ages carried out by recent generations. It may be said without exaggeration that the classical concept of the Renaissance has long since been punctured by research. We have one of the most tangible proofs of this in the use of the word 'renaissance' itself. Certain historians have envisaged a whole series of 'renaissances', the first at the time of Charlemagne and the last corresponding to the traditional period of the Renaissance, the fifteenth and sixteenth centuries. The use of the word may be said to have become accepted in relation to two of these earlier periods: the 'Carolingian Renaissance' of the ninth century, and 'the twelfth-century Renaissance'. It is, however, clear that the concept has here been given different meanings – a useful reminder that all our historical concepts are merely labels by which we seek to summarize an idea. No absolute meaning attaches to the word 'renaissance' itself; the decisive factor in our context is the reappraisal of the Middle Ages reflected in the new manner of employing the concept. Once it is understood that the concept itself contains no absolute reality, it matters very little whether we wish to reserve it for the period long referred to by that name or whether we wish to extend its use to other periods. In any case, the fact that the concept may no longer be used simply in its restrictive meaning shows a better understanding of the Middle Ages. We must considerably qualify the concept.

When we speak of the twelfth-century Renaissance we are not thinking of renaissance in the same way as was Burckhardt, but as a rebirth, a flowering, arising to be sure out of something inherited but by reason of a new initiative peculiar to the period concerned. Earlier generations, it is true, had the same heritage but without the accompanying intellectual activity. The word 'renaissance' itself presupposes a heritage taken up and re-vitalized by a new creative effort. In the context of our culture, we can only concern ourselves with the heritage of Antiquity. It must therefore be accepted – in the newer use of the concept – that such a combination of imitation and new initiative was not kept waiting until the fifteenth century but came into being more than once during the Middle Ages. This is not to say that Burckhardt's viewpoint has become unimportant, nor does it mean that we must renounce any attempt to speak of the 'Middle Ages' in the sense of trying to establish the features which – although varied – are common to the greater part of this long period in the history of Europe. But it does mean that the Middle Ages are brought closer to us. The period no longer remains merely the gloomy background to a glorious account of the rebirth of Antiquity, preparing the way for the new period: our Europe! On the contrary, it becomes an essential link in the development that has created our own world. Of course, no one would deny that the Middle Ages were formative for our own world in a banal sense, in that the period precedes the centuries that have shaped our present conditions. But the reappraisal that has taken place has made clear the extent to which the Middle Ages themselves played a decisive role in the formation of the traditions upon which later periods have continued to build.

What is the feature of the period that has caused us to use the expression 'the twelfth-century Renaissance'? Very briefly, it is the revival of the study of Roman law and Greek philosophy, with an emphasis on dialectic. There was however a flowering in all spheres of intellectual life. During this period, the new science that it is customary to refer to as early scholasticism was born. The monastic movement took on a new form, and a new piety, strongly influenced by the desire for subjective experience and understanding of the reality of faith, thrived behind the monastery walls. Intellectual growth in the twelfth century was however by no means limited to churchmen. It was also the golden age of the poetry of chivalry, and in France the study of ancient thought was revived in a manner extending far beyond theological interests. In a strange way, there was a new dedication of tradition, thereby transforming it. This desire for dedication was expressed, in relation to the Christian faith, in the striving towards intellectual understanding and the longing for personal experience. The new science and the new piety were therefore not factors appearing independently of one another, but links in one and the same movement. Tradition had now been given such a stable form that it became possible to attempt independent discussion of it. To be able to see the significance of the new factors, we must now take a glance backwards.

It is customary to look upon the intellectual life and teaching methods of the early Middle Ages as manifestations of shocking barbarism compared with ancient times. It is of course true that the collapse of the Roman Empire during the barbarian invasions caused much to decay, but the Germanic peoples by their migrations were drawn fully into the circle of Graeco-Roman culture that had already for centuries exerted an influence upon them. There is no doubt that they were not ready to bear the responsibilities forced upon them in taking over the practical administration of previously Roman areas and the Roman imperial concept itself, and it is well known that the Church was forced to take over in these restless times; indeed it was in many ways equipped for this. Neither should it be forgotten that the Rome which was overrun by the barbarians was Christian Rome. In spite of all, there was continuity. The mediaeval society that took shape after the numerous upheavals consequently had many of its roots in the world of Antiquity. This tends to emphasize that we should not over-stress the distinction between the ancient and mediaeval worlds. But there is yet another factor we might well consider before we use too gloomy colours for our picture.

It is not difficult to see the gulf between the Greek schools of philosophy or Cicero's circle on the one hand and the teaching methods at the time of Charlemagne on the other. If we use this yardstick, words like 'barbarization' and 'decay' immediately and forcibly arise. The comparison is however completely mistaken, because the basis is incorrect. The teaching methods of the early Middle Ages were not built upon those of the golden age of Antiquity but upon the methods of late Antiquity. Research into the rhetorical schools of the fourth century has now shown that formalism and traditionalism, considered as essential basic characteristics of the intellectual physiognomy, are by no means the result of the Church's influence but are a link in the heritage that it was left to the Church to administer.[1] If we consider these factors for a moment, the distance between late Antiquity and the early Middle Ages immediately becomes less great, although we must accept that it does not disappear. It is not our intention in these comments to deny that the subsequent centuries are in many ways characterized by decay, but to point out that the break is perhaps not quite so violent as is often suggested.

The Middle Ages took over their curriculum from Antiquity in the programme expressed as the seven *artes liberales*, 'the seven liberal arts'. These originally formed the basis of philosophical teaching, but in late Antiquity they became identified with total knowledge. They included on the one hand the linguistic sciences: grammar, rhetoric and dialectic (called the *trivium*), and on the other the mathematical sciences, arithmetic, geometry, music and astronomy (called the *quadrivium*). Directives for the content and use of these sciences were derived in part from the Roman writer Varro, and in part from a number of sixth-century Christian writers who preserved in their writings the ancient tradition of learning. We refer here to Boethius (*c*. 480–524), Cassiodorus (*c*. 490–583) and Isidore of Seville (*c*. 560–636). Apart from these, Augustine of Hippo (353–430) also bears mention in this connection. They are all important sources of our knowledge of ancient thought and teaching tradition in the early Middle Ages. In this period, the *artes liberales* once more took their place as preliminary instruction, but now as preparation for the study of the Bible. This, for example, was clearly their position in Charlemagne's ecclesiastical legislation, which incorporated a programme of higher education that itself became the standard for later centuries. This position for the *artes* followed of course from the fact that the object of higher education was to train priests. Certain of these sciences had however a tendency in practice to evade this subordinate position. An example of this was rhetoric, which had understandably to tempt its students into the practice of it, even when no higher purpose was thereby served. As we shall see, dialectic also possessed these possibilities.

The Carolingian Renaissance, which is closely associated with the Emperor's great efforts towards educational reform, is with one notable exception (John Scotus Erigena, died *c*. 870) characterized not by original thinkers but by intensive study and much collection of material from Antiquity and the Fathers. This was a revival of past eras only in so far as it took the form of a reproduction. A Belgian historian (J. de Ghellinck) has pointed out that all this diligence led in the main to the scientific and religious luggage of the past being registered. Alongside this reproduction, there was some endeavour in the field of dialectic. Nevertheless, we should not give the period too low an assessment. Later periods were able to benefit from and to build upon the tradition of learning established. There was a review of all knowledge, and the first hesitant attempts were made to systematize it. The lines were laid down for the work of later centuries.

If we consider theology, which was in fact the principal aim, it consisted mainly of biblical interpretation through glosses; that is to say short textual explanations in the form of an exegesis of individual words and concepts. Until as late as the eleventh century, the systematic effort generally extended no further than the assembly of quotations from the Fathers of the ancient Church in the so-called *florilegia,* collections of brief statements concerning the truths of the Christian faith. Dialectic was the most important of the profane sciences. It included linguistic logic – the theory of the meaning of words and sentences – and what is referred to as formal logic – the theory of the correct manner of drawing conclusions. Boethius was the great authority on this. Most notably, he made available through translations into Latin important sections of Aristotelian logic. He also wrote a series of commentaries on Aristotle and other ancient writers, and in addition there were his own logical writings.

On the face of it, there is nothing very remarkable in the 'renaissance' character of the Carolingian epoch. And yet it deserves the title because all its endeavour in the service of tradition was focused towards a definite correlation of the strands of knowledge. Perhaps in the final analysis this is the true renaissancelike characteristic of the period. Charlemagne and his scholars did not act as they did for incidental reasons. All their work in the service of teaching and scholarship was consciously regarded as a link in the recreation of the Roman Empire, which found its political expression in Charlemagne's unification of the Western countries, followed by his coronation as Emperor.

During the period immediately after the Carolingian Renaissance, a fairly clear distinction was maintained between the *artes liberales* and theology, but in the eleventh century there was a marked drawing together. Higher education was provided in the cathedral schools and in certain monastic schools. A number of these schools now blossomed forth, particularly in France. This is true of the cathedral schools in Paris, Rheims, Tours, Laon, Chartres and many others, and also of the monastic school at Bec in Normandy. These schools became centres of scholarship, and from them came the first attempts to escape from slavish adherence to the traditions of the past. In particular, an increased interest in dialectic and its theological application can be observed. Theology concentrated entirely on the conservation of the tradition of the Fathers, and the importance of dialectic was restricted mainly to providing the necessary definitions of the meaning of words and concepts. But as soon as the interest in dialectic that arose in the second half of the eleventh century had emancipated itself it was well on the way to a renewed consideration of the traditional theological material from a logical point of view. This is in fact what occurred. In some places theological interest receded into the background in favour of dialectic as an independent occupation, but it was not long before dialectic began to be employed in the consideration of theological problems. This interest provoked fierce resistance in conservative circles, and it may be said that the last half of the century was marked by a conflict over the function of dialectic between dialecticians and anti-dialecticians. The environment can probably best be illustrated by some concrete examples.

The best known and possibly most impressive example of this conflict is the so-called Berengarian Eucharistic dispute. Berengar (died 1088), who taught at the cathedral school of Tours, was a professed supporter of the use of dialectic in theology. In his Eucharistic writings, reason was put forward as the opponent of authority, and Berengar did not hesitate to assert that he considered reason, represented by dialectic, to be superior to Church doctrine. Opposition to him was strong, and it was this very opposition that was to influence the period immediately following. The conviction that Berengar's conception of the Eucharist was heretical caused many people to condemn the tool he had employed – dialectic. In addition, its use in practice often led to an empty delight in dispute; for example by the well-known Anselm of Besate, called the Peripatetic. This designation had been applied since ancient times to the followers of Aristotle, but it also fits Anselm quite literally. He was in fact a wandering philosopher, travelling all over Europe in constant search of people with whom he might dispute. His type could readily arouse illwill towards dialectic on the part of conservative theologians.

The best known representative of the conservative view is Peter Damian (1006/7–1072). He played a considerable part in the movement for Church reform, which sought by all available means to free the Church of worldly influence. He was a zealous castigator of all symptoms of decline within the Church and a keen advocate of ascetic piety as the means towards a restoration of the Church. In the very same manner as can later be observed in Bernard of Clairvaux, his striving after personal piety was associated with a clear politico-ecclesiastical aim, showing no scruple in the use of force against all those who, in his opinion, were obstacles to the work of reformation. He was not only opposed to the use of dialectic in theology, but also to profane science in general. For Damian, the natural world was saturated with sin, and consequently the only worthy attitude was to flee from the world. It was he who formulated the catch phrase that philosophy is justified only as the handmaid of theology, *ancilla theologiae*. Confronted with theological cognition, even logic must give way. According to Damian, the omnipotence of God is not bound by the principle of contradiction; for example, God can make the done undone. It was therefore not a far cry to the assertion of a double truth; one for theology, another for philosophy. Damian did not take this path, but condemned philosophy, viewed as an independent activity, as the sinful work of man. But Damian did not succeed in preventing the continuation of dialectic study in the schools. There were also more moderate opponents of the consequences flowing from the Berengarian Eucharistic dispute. They did not write off dialectic, but subordinated it to divine authority. One of these men was Berengar's famous opponent Lanfranc, the founder of the monastic school at Bec where his pupils included Anselm of Canterbury.

This conflict over dialectic had brought to the fore one of the problems that were inherited by the thought of later centuries: the relationship between reason and revelation, between *ratio* and *auctoritas*. But the Eucharistic dispute did not raise this problem, and it should not be overvalued on these grounds. It is rather part of the evidence that the problem had now become a burning issue. It was not new; it had been an essential theme for Augustine, who had adopted from Antiquity the concept of *auctoritas* and used it in a Christian context in relation to the authority of the Bible, the Fathers and the Church. But, at the same time, he was trying to arrive at a speculative understanding in which reason played an important part. Consequently, when mediaeval theologians began to interest themselves in demonstrating the rational nature of the faith, they were able to turn to Augustine himself, since he offered excellent examples of the use of dialectic in the service of theology.

We must stop for a moment before we continue our attempt to show how this problem was tackled around the year 1100, and in this way to understand the background to the activities of the man we are here concerned with. The pair of concepts, *auctoritas* and *ratio*, express a point highly characteristic of mediaeval thought. In one sense it is the main problem of the entire period, even during the period 800–1100, the age of reproduction and traditionalism. Sometimes it was dealt with directly, as in the case of John Scotus Erigena, but in every instance it was latent in the method of teaching current at that time. Alongside the gathering of traditional material, dialectical teaching was always evident. By the end of the eleventh century, dialectic had attained such independence that the relationship between reason and authority became a problem for everyone, irrespective of his position. A completely new situation was thereby created; the 'state of innocence' of the prevalent traditionalism was over. It was no longer taken for granted that all effort should be concentrated upon as exact a reproduction as possible of the Church Fathers, for alongside this hereditary attitude there were other viewpoints in deference to which the traditionalist had now *knowingly* to limit himself. This was a great step forward, because it forced the disputing parties to articulate their positions.

In the first phase of the dispute between dialecticians and anti-dialecticians it might appear that the problem was best expressed by a choice: reason or authority. This is an illustration of the attitude of the conservatives, the traditionalists, in relation to Berengar of Tours. But his attitude is not typical of mediaeval thought. It was customary – right up to the end of the Middle Ages – to accept the validity of authority without question, irrespective of the individual's attitude towards the relationship between reason and revelation. The problem was not whether authority was valid before the tribunal of reason, but whether and to what extent it was possible to substantiate authority on the basis of reason. Berengar was an exception, but the dispute was continued after he had been rejected by the Church. There was simply no way back to the matter-of-course traditionalism. But it is important to bear in mind that those advocating the use of dialectic in theology normally had no thought of disputing the validity of the authoritative nature of tradition. Mediaeval thinkers did not anticipate the Age of Enlightenment.

The inviolable position of the concept of authority throughout the Middle Ages has perhaps more than any other factor contributed to the formation of the impression of intellectual darkness during this period. In fact everyone was dependent upon the Church, all knowledge being limited and dominated by religious dogma, and he who tried his hand at philosophy had to reckon with the authorities! Greek philosophy, initially represented by Plato and later, to a greater degree, by Aristotle, was the basis upon which one built. Against this background, is it therefore unreasonable to look upon this millennium as a regrettable parenthesis in the history of the human intellect? It must appear so to a person with no sense of history. But once it is grasped that our whole existence can be comprehended only as historical existence things begin to look quite different. We then understand, irrespective of what we may think of a later age's clash with the concept of authority, that the road from naïve traditionalism to the eventual clash could not evade the discussion of the relationship between reason and authority that became such an essential content of scholastic thought. Consequently, on historical grounds, both the Roman Catholic who considers scholastic thought to be essentially valid even today, at least in its intention, and the so-called 'cultural radical' may regard scholasticism as an important link in the advancing development towards our own times.

Traditionalism, both in its naïve form and in the form used to fight the dialecticians, considered it to be its duty to sustain as faithfully as possible the teaching of the Fathers. It sought to perform this duty by carefully reproducing what tradition made available. But this was the very means by which the tradition it wished to protect was killed! In this connection it should be pointed out that their reproductions were only a faint reflection of the originals. Tradition is alive only when it inspires the creation of new work. As already said, those who advocated the use of dialectic in theology normally had no wish to question the authoritative nature of tradition, but they refused to kill it off merely by reproducing it. From this point of view, it may be said that the period we are here concerned with was the introduction to the revival of tradition that characterizes the following centuries, the age of scholasticism.

Apart from the dispute over dialectic, canon law also played its part in intensifying study during this period. In the latter half of the eleventh century, the centuries-long struggle between Pope and Emperor began. Among the basic reasons for this controversy, one of the most important was the religious reform movement of the tenth century, the principal aim of which was to obtain freedom for the Church; that is to say freedom of the affairs of the Church from all worldly influence. This set in motion the tremendous task of exploring and systematizing canon law. Here also it was with the authorities that the work lay. They often did not agree, and efforts were then made to arrive at an adjustment between them. In the effort to arrange and to systematize the many provisions of canon law, experience in method was gained that could be employed in theology, which of course was also concerned with authority.

All this laid the foundation for the science we refer to as scholasticism. While the traditional renaissance concept presupposes a sharp contrast between scholasticism and renaissance (humanism), it is the intellectual activity itself of which scholasticism is an expression that has given rise to the term: the twelfth-century Renaissance. There is however no doubt that the humanism of the fifteenth and sixteenth centuries saw itself as a reaction, founded upon classical literature, against the style-less and tasteless formalism of scholasticism. In spite of this, there is good reason to use the term 'renaissance' in both cases. It was merely that different aspects of the heritage of Antiquity were revived; in the twelfth century, the judical (the study of Roman Law) and philosophical (dialectic), and in the fifteenth century, the literary. The dominant position of dialectic was the decisive factor in the construction of the science of scholasticism, but it was the means by which style and taste themselves were destroyed. This in turn evoked the literary anti-mediaeval renaissance of the fifteenth century.

It is apparent that many significant nuances have been disregarded in this characterization; only those factors that first catch the eye have been brought out. As is always the case, the reality was infinitely richer and more varied than is apparent from our attempt to make it comprehensible. For example, much literary activity is also to be found in the twelfth century. The schools at Orleans and Chartres were famous for their teaching of 'grammar', which included a thorough study of ancient literature. Nor did the period lack new poetry, both worldly and religious, some in the style of the classics and some in new forms. In the long run, however, it became difficult for this interest in classical literature to assert itself in the face of the strong competition created by the new translations of Aristotle. By the middle of the century his entire logic was available in Latin, and translations of his other works soon followed. Work upon this enormous amount of material now attracted the attention of almost all intellectuals, and classical studies declined fast in popularity. It was the revival of dialectic and judicial studies that was to characterize the following centuries.

Before we try to analyse more closely the characteristics of early scholasticism, it would be as well to take a look at its social and economic background; we have been concerned so far mainly with the intellectual background. A peculiarity of the environment of study around the year 1100, that is to say at the time scholasticism seriously commenced, was that the new activity throve almost exclusively in the cathedral schools, while the monastic schools that had dominated the field in the previous century rapidly lost significance. The monastic school at Bec was at the end of the eleventh century the last monastic school of importance in the flowering of the sciences. The circumstances are so marked that there is reason to ask why this happened. A Russian scholar, N. A. Sidorova, in a treatise on Abelard (which as concerns Abelard's thought is more confusing than informative) has set out viewpoints of a socio-economic nature in accordance with Soviet Russian dogma. It is asserted that Abelard's background was in the development of the towns – a feature in contrast to feudal society. Abelard is here interpreted as a representative of *la première civilisation citadine en France* and the proceedings against him, particularly those initiated by Bernard of Clairvaux, are seen as the reaction of the feudal Church against this new culture. Apart from this the treatise has no interest, but it must be conceded that the sugges-tion itself gives expression to a point of substance.[2] The religious reform movement was mainly inspired by the monasteries, and it is interesting that the Cluniacs and their contemporaries were tied to the feudal system of society. In the struggle for the free-dom of the Church, the innate secular bias of the sciences and of literature had been taken for granted, and for this reason these intellectual pursuits were looked upon with suspicion by the reformers. The Cistercian Order, the most important twelfth-century innovation within the monastic movement, had no school for anyone but the monks, and study as such formed no part of the programme of the Order. In the twelfth century the initiative passed to other hands and the monasteries were left in isolation, which was certainly better suited to their purposes; it was in the cathedral schools in the cities that study flourished. It is clear that the social circumstance behind this development was the advancing urbanization of society. In twelfth-century France, a tangible expression of this was the struggle of the municipalities for independence from both spiritual and worldly masters. In this environment, study was given a far wider purpose than it had had in the monasteries, where it had always been subordinate to the spirit of monastic life. This development was strengthened by advancing centralization. As early as the beginning of the century, we find the most important centres of study located in Francia, that is to say in the area around Paris, and with Abelard Paris attained an absolute leading position for the first time.[3]

These new schools gave rise to an intellectual environment that was somewhat removed from the programme of the re-formed Orders. The monasteries consequently became the strongholds of conservatism and traditionalism, while it was the cathedral schools that gave birth to 'the twelfth-century Renais-sance'. These schools provided the foundation for the great mediaeval movement in the development of scholarly life – the universities. No contribution whatever was made to this by the various monastic and canonical reforms. This is not to imply that individual persons active in these circles did not contribute. Some of them did so, even considerably, but as a movement their reaction to the new intellectual activity was no more than a powerless attempt to arrest the questioning that was to set in motion enormous spiritual forces. Similarly, the type of society they represented was to be overcome by the *bourgeoisie*.

To summarize, it may be said that two features were combined in early scholasticism. On the one hand, there was the attempt, with the help of dialectic, to master the substance of faith in the form of understanding. On the other hand, the recognition of the differences between the many traditional authorities, first perceived in canon law, impelled the scholastics towards systematic arrangement and summarization. In both cases the concept of authority, itself unquestioned, produced a number of problems whose solution appeared to be imperative. The new complex of problems caused the work of the schools to be greatly intensified and created new literary forms in scientific investigation. The scholastic *quaestio* was created. This word is characteristic of the situation, because now the manifold areas covered by traditional dogma came themselves to be questioned. The manner of this was not to doubt their truth, but to acknowledge that in many cases there were difficulties to be cleared away before what had been inherited from the Fathers could be re-confirmed. In teaching, the so-called *lectio* had since olden times played the main part. It consisted of a type of lecture on one book or another that was read aloud paragraph by paragraph and commented upon, following the gloss method. Now another working method appropriate to the new manner of presenting a problem was added to this: *disputatio*, in which it was sought to penetrate a problem by logical analysis in conversational form.[4]

The first to give original expression to the new endeavours was Anselm of Canterbury (1033/34–1109). He considered it his task, accepting the basic truth of authority, to trace the foundation of faith, the rationale of faith. His programme is clearly expressed in the following often-quoted words from the introduction to the treatise *Proslogion*: 'I do not seek, oh Lord, to penetrate Your sublimity, as I in no way compare my understanding therewith; but I desire to some extent to understand

Your truth, which my heart believes and loves. That is to say, I do not seek to understand so that I may believe, but I believe so that I may understand.'[5] Faith for Anselm therefore was an absolute pre-condition of understanding. On another occasion he rejected any discussion concerning the truth and reality of faith. What could and must be investigated, however, is *why* this *is* so. If this can be understood, God is to be thanked; if it is impossible, one must bow down in adoration.[6] Against this background, it comes as no surprise that authority was Anselm's unshakable starting point. Nevertheless, direct references to the authorities are to be found with surprising rarity in his writings. This is precisely where he demonstrated that he differed profoundly from earlier theologians, who had concerned themselves primarily with assembling the authorities. This difference is associated with Anselm's conscious striving to go beyond the available information. He wished to achieve a rational insight into the content of faith and to solve the difficulties arising from a speculative preoccupation with the truth of faith. It was consequently necessary to reach beyond faith as found in the Bible and in the Church Fathers, and it was therefore natural that the proofs of Holy Writ and of the Fathers could not form the substance of Anselm's writings.

He made use essentially of two methods to arrive at the desired insight. First, he sought, following Augustine's example, to comprehend God by a speculative immersion in the analogies of the divine in Creation, particularly rational Creation. The more the rational intellect immerses itself, the more it understands the God whose image it is.[7] The other method was a theological development of logic. Anselm had received a thorough dialectical training at Lanfranc's school. His writings bear witness to a wide familiarity with Aristotle, in so far as he was known at that time. The dialectical orientation is shown in the care taken to define the concept precisely and in his predilection for dialogue.[8] The significance of this theological platform is principally remarkable in that here for the first time expression was given to what was to be the aspiration of scholasticism: to reach, on the basis of Church authority, a thoroughly rational understanding of the mysteries of faith. Viewed in a later historical perspective, Anselm's importance for subsequent times lies in his revitalizing tradition by using it as a starting point instead of repeating it. The complex of problems that determined his theological work was already current, but he was the first to succeed in giving shape to what at the time existed only in the form of trends and attempts – to such a degree that posterity found the path already marked out.

But this is not to say that his theological method was taken over directly by the scholastic theologians. It is true that his pupils became the most influential teachers during the early decades of the twelfth century, but they had not the stature of their master, and they met their superior in one of their own pupils, Peter Abelard. In his autobiography, he has drawn a picture of the famous teachers of his youth, Anselm of Laon and William of Champeaux. These two theologians were well chosen to emphasize his own importance, but he probably did not do them sufficient justice. There is no doubt that Abelard was the superior of both these men, but at the same time he used their work as a basis, developed their methods and led them on to victory. The German historical theologian, Reinhold Seeberg, has made a comparison between Anselm of Canterbury and Abelard which is worth considering. For both men, the problem is the relationship between *ratio* and *auctoritas*. But whereas Anselm saw Church doctrine more as the Church's historical purpose in its entirety, Abelard considered particularly the individual dogmas valid in canon law. Anselm employed both the Bible and the authority of the Fathers to the extent that he identified himself with the ideas he considered representative, and thereafter he worked on from this basis. But for Abelard the authorities appeared everywhere as individual statements which could be played off against one another, so that the task became one of mitigating and overcoming incompatibilities.[9] This method has its quintessence in one of Abelard's treatises: *Sic et non*; that is, Yes and No. In the prologue to this, Abelard gives directions for the evaluation and discussion of conflicting authorities. He gives particular weight to the consideration of incompatibilities by linguistic analysis: are they real or do they merely rest on the different use of words? Apart from this, he lays down rules for examining the genuineness and the degree of commitment of the authorities; the authority of the Bible stands above all others. It is clear that this conception gave great latitude to dialectic.

It would be wrong however to conclude from this that Abelard's intentions were in line with those of a man like Berengar of Tours. As we shall see, he was highly aware of the dangers that might flow from too great a confidence in dialectical ability. For Abelard also, Church dogma was the unquestionable basis. He had no wish to place dialectic above theology, but by its use he wished to understand revelation as far as is possible and to reconcile incompatibilities. The history of the period shows that this typical mediaeval subordination to authority, theological as well as philosophical, in no way signified a narrowing of the opportunities for thought, as might be believed on the basis of our assumptions. It was true that the authorities were indisputable, but they could and must be interpreted. Herein lay the opportunity. In certain fields, particularly in grammar and in the literary forms of expression, authority might lead to servility to the model, but in theology and philosophy interpretation presented an opportunity for an infinity of nuances.

The difference between Abelard and Anselm was of course largely determined by their individual talents, but their different careers also contributed to this. For Anselm of Canterbury, theological study was bound up with the contemplative life. Prayer, meditation and theology formed one whole. Although he reached high office, he remained the monk who in his search for God yearned also for that insight which even in life could grant him a foretaste of heavenly glory. Abelard's starting point is quite different. His faculty for the higher studies was recognized early on. From the outset he was the professional scholar whose ambition was to have his own school. In the matter of theological study, he was convinced that whoever knew the craft – that is dialectic – was the possessor of the most important equipment. The rest was merely reading the necessary works, that is to say the Bible and the Fathers. The profession was the starting point, which tells us nothing whatever about Abelard's relationship to the Church. What it does show, however, is that his entry into the field is of a different nature from that of Anselm of Canterbury. In this sense, Abelard is a *school theologian* in a manner quite different from Anselm. This is due not only to psychological differences between the two, but also to the simple fact that external conditions had changed between Anselm's youth and Abelard's youth. Scholasticism was now a reality in the sense that, cutting across all intellectual movements and currents, cutting across all private motives and desires, there existed an academic climate, so to speak, with competing scholastic traditions and intellectual ambitions.

It is not intended here to suggest that Anselm, as a type, is only conceivable before the foundation of the schools took on a true professional character; on the contrary, the subsequent history of scholasticism continued to display a wealth of nuances impossible to summarize into formulae. It is rather the intention to point out that Abelard's entry into theological study was in no way an expression of irreligious and so-called liberal thought; all this was alien to him. But the development of the original scholastic theology about the year 1100 made his attitude *possible* without interfering with other attitudes, all within the framework of the Church. It might perhaps be said that Abelard personified more than many others what was *new*, introduced by scholastic theology – in its capacity as a professional activity – into the intellectual life of the period. This he did, on the one hand, on the strength of his eminent ability – it was impossible not to notice him – but on the other hand, he was perhaps more responsible for developments than many because some of the other great names of the period, while remaining scholastic theologians, carried on with the old pursuits to a greater extent than he. This was the position with a number of theologians who were monks first and foremost. In the case of Abelard, the 'modern' trends were quite undisguised by old and long-acknowledged features. It is probably correct to see in this fact part of the explanation for the offence he so deeply gave, particularly among the supporters of monastic reform.

In these circles the attitude was quite different. We may take as an example the man who was to become Abelard's great opponent, Bernard of Clairvaux. We have emphasized earlier the great difference between Anselm of Canterbury and Abelard. But although Bernard turned upon Abelard with every weapon at his disposal, it would be wrong to think that he felt

akin to Anselm. This was in no way true. If we look more
closely at his conception of theology and science, it soon becomes
clear that he was forced to react to Abelard as he did.[10] Bernard
was no opponent of theology, but he fixed very definite limits
for it. Theology should not concern itself with knowing everything possible but should concentrate on the only thing important to Bernard: the understanding of God and self. Knowledge
for the sake of knowledge he considered to be empty curiosity.
He therefore had little time for philosophy. It led easily to
arrogance, and therefore away from the knowledge of salvation,
which cannot be acquired without humility. To reduce theological thought to a question of dialectical ability seemed to him
outrageous, since it is of the Holy Ghost and is therefore not
determined simply by human reason; understanding and love
cannot be separated.

In his opinions, Bernard was thoroughly conservative; he
wished to protect tradition and to be simple and yet cautious in
all theological statements. He usually preferred to express himself in biblical terms, and he would not venture into speculation
that was too lofty for him. It was not for man to concern himself with the exploration of God's majesty, but merely to be
eager to know His will. Bernard wished not so much to explain
as to fertilize the heart. He therefore had misgivings about
Anselm of Canterbury's method of pursuing theology. The
question for him was whether the insight Anselm strove after
can be found at all on earth. We live in the shadow of faith;
Bernard believed therefore not so much in understanding as in
yearning and love. His dislike of Abelard arose from his method
of study: speculation and curiosity makes man forget man himself, that is to say the knowledge that is his only concern – the
understanding of his true position in relation to God. It is natural
that Bernard found it difficult to come to terms with the
developments in the field of theology during his lifetime.

We have tried to indicate here the lines of demarcation within
twelfth-century thought in a brief survey of the most important
viewpoints, as they appeared to Anselm of Canterbury, Abelard
and Bernard. This should not be taken to represent completely
the individual opinions of these theologians; there were in fact

very wide-spread variations in all three cases. History today often distinguishes between 'scholastic' and 'monastic' theology. The latter concept has carried weight in recent years, and it may be appropriate, in connection with the conflicts of the twelfth century, to explain in rather more detail what is meant by this. It should be possible in this way to pursue and develop from a slightly different aspect the considerations necessary to understand the 'renaissance' that have been put forward above.

A natural starting point is perhaps the dispute already referred to between dialecticians and anti-dialecticians that marked the latter half of the eleventh century. The opposition came particularly from those monks who saw in the ever-growing influence of dialectic a wrong turning, an emancipation of thought. The theology practised in the monasteries until then – and this means in general all existing theology – had a quite definite purpose: to serve monastic life. The new version, originating largely in the cathedral schools, had however an intellectual bias which was alien to the older theology. In the twelfth century, therefore, two types of theology existed alongside one another, sometimes in conflict but always different in purpose, although it must be appreciated that the transitions are gradual. In the thirteenth century, scholasticism stood out as the victor, no longer with any 'monastic' theology of importance at its side. This is partly because there was no longer a monastic culture that could compete in intensity and originality with that of the twelfth century, but it was also because the 'new' theology, scholasticism, was no longer new and therefore no longer an object of suspicion to the monks. Indeed, they themselves and the friars supplied most of the great teachers of high scholasticism.

If we now look at Anselm of Canterbury against this background, he must be regarded as a typical transitional figure. He stemmed from the famous monastery school at Bec and his theology had a pronounced purpose of personal contemplation, although he employed to a high degree the aids regarded with suspicion by the conservatives. He therefore stood outside the sharp differentiation that was to be witnessed later, but this placing is also perhaps why he had no significant *direct* influence during the period immediately following. Bernard had no use for him, and his own pupils became scholastics in the true sense.

But how then can we characterize more closely the difference between scholastic and monastic theology? It can perhaps be seen most clearly in the critics of the new theology, for example Rupert of Deutz (c. 1070–1129) who compared the new schools with Christ's school, *schola Christi*. What exasperated him was the objectification that arose – that is, the scientific purpose itself; the aim was to find causes and reasons. For Rupert, there was only one reason (*ratio*) of importance – the will of God. In the new endeavours he saw a profanation of *sacra pagina*, Holy Scripture, and therefore of revelation. In *schola Christi* there is no place for syllogisms, he said. Another opponent of the new theology put out a treatise under the heading: 'Concerning God's Prescience Towards the Curious', in which another substantial accusation from the 'monastic' side was put forward: one stands amazed before the attempt to defend the faith rationally; it remains a mystery, not analogous to this world and its wisdom. From the monastic viewpoint, nature and history can never have intrinsic value, but can at the most be used symbolically in the service of a higher cause. This is something quite different from what occurs in scholasticism. As monks – although still on earth – live their life in heaven, the earthly can have significance for them only in the form of an image, that is to say as a symbol of heavenly reality.[11]

Monastic theology differed from the scholastic not only in its purpose but also in its method; and finally, it may be added, in its sources.[12] In both camps there was of course study of the Bible and of the Fathers, but the scholastics added the pagan philosophers to this. In the monasteries they had no use for these; the Bible clearly occupied first place. We must remember, however, that the Bible was never studied as an isolated literary document but parallel with a living and historical tradition; its environment, so to say, was that of the liturgy. We must also remember that all monks at that time, before the mendicant Orders were founded, were choir monks. This cardinal point of monastic life was predetermined by a number of texts, with the monastic Rules of Benedict and Basil in the fore. Apart from this, many monasteries possessed a rich assortment of the Latin and Greek Fathers. Although knowledge of the Greek language was slight, what was referred to as the 'light of the East' (*orientale lumen*) had never been forgotten in the monasteries. It is, however, certain that, in monastic theology particularly, the old Latin translations of the Greek provided new inspiration in the twelfth century. The translations of Origen were particularly important.

This whole background caused the monks to be attracted most to that scholastic theology which was of a traditional character. Examination of the German libraries of the period has shown that the scholastic texts most frequently represented in the monasteries of the twelfth century were those of Anselm of Laon, William of Champeaux and Hugh of St Victor. All three were regular canons; that is to say they lived a communal life which in general offered similar living conditions to those of the monks. People therefore tended to gather around those whose teaching had a patristic character; that is, was founded upon the Fathers. Monks were critical of Abelard and his contemporary Gilbert de la Porrée – even of Anselm of Canterbury – and did not seek to read their works. There is no doubt that the position in the libraries is expressive of a clear choice.

The monks saw the Christian sources, the Bible and the Fathers, as no more than instruments in their yearning to reach the source of life itself, the living faith. Consequently they were not concerned with explaining the dogma and drawing conclusions by means of dialectic, but with salvation, the unity of man with God, which was their vocation. They concentrated their attention upon the life of Jesus, upon the Church and upon the Eucharist. They wished to attain perfect love, which is the fulfilment of the law. Everything else, even the dogma itself, were no more than means. The many tracts *De caritate* (concerning love) consequently characterize monastic theology of the twelfth century. In this they found no help in Aristotle's logic, but turned more towards Origen and Augustine.

Finally, the method was also different from that of scholasticism. Indeed, one can scarcely speak of a method. Scholasticism was characterized by speculation and abstraction; monastic theology by concrete experience. Scholasticism was analytical;

it proceeded from point to point in an advancing movement of thought. Monastic theology was distinctly synthetic; it always had the whole aim in mind and did not become bogged down in detail; it reduced everything to the unique mystery, God, Who is love revealed in Christ. Consequently, prayer and meditation were its true elements, and it did not constantly seek, as did scholasticism, to expand the range of its understanding. Intellectual activity was dominated by *affectus*, the impassioned search for God which alone legitimized it.

The contrast we have here tried to explain belongs in the theological field. The people of the reform movement might well regard with suspicion the great academic activity then current in philosophy and literature. They might try as best they could to suppress these occupations in the monasteries, but it was first and foremost the new theology that aroused their wrath. The most surprising manifestation of this is that in the twelfth century it was to be neither the renewed interest in nature nor the intensive preoccupation with classical writers that raised doubts about tradition; it was, in particular, theology. At the beginning of the century, natural science was at a very low level, but during the following period the Greek mathematicians, scientists and doctors were translated into Latin. A number of Arabic works followed later. By about 1250, the Latin world was in possession of almost the entire achievement of Antiquity as well as of Islam in these fields. But however much this new knowledge may have contributed to an understanding of nature, it represented no revolution in the understanding of man and his world. We have strong proof of the spread of classical education in contemporary letter writing, in itself a typical 'renaissance' feature.[13] As in the fifteenth and sixteenth centuries, letter writing was cultivated as an art; one imitated the classical writers and demonstrated one's knowledge of them by numerous quotations. Letters became objects of great collector interest, and cultured people of the time formed collections of their letters, both sent and received.[14] Even pious monks were not unaffected by this atmosphere. In one sense it is justifiable to speak of a humanistic current within intellectual life of the period, but it became more of an ornament, a studied elegance, than a Christian element. People amused themselves with a little innocent worldliness without allowing this is any way to prejudice the religious interpretation of life.

It should however be added that this worldliness was not always quite so innocent. It is completely wrong to imagine that intellectual life in the Middle Ages, under 'the dominating influence of the Church', presented an image similar in some respects to our picture of the golden age of Puritanism in England after the fall of Charles I, or of life in Calvin's Geneva. Some of the poetry of the twelfth century, for example, is nothing less than shocking even to our hardened senses. The same men wrote hymns for the Church and drinking songs that in coarseness and worldly greed have scarcely been surpassed. Satire flourished, and nothing was sacred to it. Ovid was one of the most popular of the ancient writers.[16] All this, however, led to no crisis. It is rather proof of how undisputed was the basic attitude of the Church. This is also true of the distinct disposition towards blasphemy often expressed in the literary products of the period, particularly in poems and songs. This was an abreaction, so to speak, against what no one for a moment would have considered toppling from its supremacy.

It was quite a different matter when a theologian identified with the renaissance used the new knowledge to formulate new questions in relation to the traditional dogmas. In these circumstances it was possible for classical literature, the new understanding of nature and, most of all, dialectic to lead to a collision with the advocates of tradition. Among the thinkers of the twelfth century, there is scarcely any better person than Peter Abelard to illustrate these conflicts. By virtue of his stature and his importance to later generations he is one of the most characteristic personalities of the renaissance. Apart from this, his life story, which will be told in the following pages, provides a colourful and varied picture of academic and religious life in the first half of the twelfth century.

CHAPTER 2

The Young Dialectician

The main source of our knowledge of Abelard's life is his autobiography, *Historia calamitatum suarum* 'The Story of his Misfortunes'. This little treatise in the form of a letter was written at
the beginning of the 1130s. At that time his situation was somewhat miserable, and this affects his manner of looking back on
his stormy life. Fortunately we can at a number of points supple-
ment the knowledge made available to us in the autobiography
by information from other quarters. There are for example a
small number of letters to and from Abelard, and he was such a
remarkable person that he is mentioned in a number of contemporary letters and accounts. But in spite of this there remain certain gaps in our knowledge of his career; we must often be content with assumptions that we are unable to confirm from the
sources. The autobiography, which he professes to have been
written to a friend to console him in his misery, is remarkable for
the frankness and ruthlessness with which the author reveals his
own errors. This however does not prevent its being at the
same time supported by much egotism and – undeniably – self-
pity. When we know more of Abelard's fate, we shall be wary
about passing judgment on him for this reason. It is difficult not
to feel discomfort at the unshakable self-confidence he displays.
If he is to be believed, it had been difficult for him all through his
life to find his equal on an academic level. He had always been
the victor; others had always been forced to give in to his superi-

ority and, for this reason, they had always become envious of him and had vented their resentment in unjust persecution. Can this be true? Strange to say, Abelard's statements are, in this respect, largely confirmed by much contemporary evidence from both friend and foe.[1] It appears to be true that he never had the experience of meeting an equal opponent and that his personality and teaching had a public attraction previously unknown. That envy is the reason for the negative reactions to this is of course Abelard's personal interpretation, and only his friends were able to agree with him here. It is however indisputable that his presence always gave cause for strife. Controversy was simply his true element. When he was finally overcome, it was not under his conditions – in an academic dispute – but by an agency in the face of which he was powerless: the personal influence of Saint Bernard. We shall return to this later. For the moment we shall follow Abelard's career up to the time when, through his meeting with Heloïse, he was diverted from his course.

Abelard was born in 1079 in the town of Le Pallet in Brittany, not far from Nantes. His father, Berengar, was a knight in the service of the Count of Brittany. His mother's name was Lucia. We know almost nothing of Abelard's childhood. He himself writes that his father had some education and that he took great care over his sons' upbringing and education. Peter was the eldest and therefore heir to the father's vassal rights. But when he had received his initial instruction in scholarship, in which he made rapid and easy progress, he completely renounced his father's way of life: 'I was overcome by such a love of scholarship that I left to my brothers the glory and honours of war together with my inheritance and the right of primogeniture and broke away completely from the Courts of Mars to be raised in the lap of Minerva. I preferred the warfare of dialectical methods to all other teachings in philosophy, and so I exchanged military weapons for others and set the battles of verbal dispute above the trophies of war. I therefore travelled through many provinces in order to dispute, and I appeared as an imitator of the Peripatetics wherever I heard that this art was eagerly cultivated.'[2] These words from the autobiography not only inform us of Abelard's decision to choose a different career from that of his family but also illuminate remarkably the environment of study when Abelard was a young man.

Although the seven *artes liberales* were the accepted basis for all higher education, it must not be imagined that all these arts were cultivated to the same degree by every student and in every school. Abelard's account, as we know from many other sources, comes much nearer to the truth. Each person chose a special field for himself, and to study it he had to seek those schools where he could expect to increase his knowledge in that field specifically.[8] From the age of fifteen or perhaps even earlier Abelard was presumably one of the wandering 'scholars'. It was the masters of dialectic he sought. We know that throughout his life his knowledge of mathematics was quite small, and it is probable that he was in general very little interested in the so-called real sciences, the *quadrivium*. His interest concentrated upon the *trivium*, the rational disciplines. Grammar and rhetoric were the labels under which classical literature was studied. In these he was well versed, but he gave first place to the senior of the *trivium*, dialectic. Unfortunately we have little information as to the schools he visited in his early youth before reaching Paris, although one of the first places he resided at must have been the town of Loches where one of the most famous dialecticians of the time, Roscelin, was teaching. He had led a tumultuous life. Because of the consequences of his dialectic upon the teaching concerning the Trinity he had fallen foul of the Church authorities, and for the rest of his life he remained a somewhat suspicious personage in the eyes of his contemporaries. When Abelard later appeared in public he always tried clearly to disassociate himself from Roscelin, although he made no attempt to conceal that he had been his pupil. Roscelin's reputation is probably the reason for his not being mentioned in the autobiography in this context.[4]

We may assume that Abelard's travels brought him nearer and nearer to Paris. He arrived probably around the year 1100, but it is not possible to be precise in this. He writes that the art of dialectic 'already then' flourished mostly in that city. The foremost master was the respected William of Champeaux, Archdeacon of Notre Dame. He was a pupil of Anselm of Laon, and alongside him the most important name in the French academic world at that time. Abelard, who is otherwise not very generous in praising his contemporaries, writes that he was 'justly' considered the most outstanding figure in dialectic. As the centre of Capetian power, Paris had a natural advantage in attaining the leading position in scholarship, and there is no doubt that William had increased the reputation of the school. It must be assumed that when Abelard arrived it was already held in such esteem that only Chartres among the provincial schools could contend for precedence with it. Some people believe that Abelard before his residence in Paris had been at Chartres for some time, but we have no certain knowledge about this. At all events it was natural that Paris and not Chartres should become his actual domicile as a pupil and a teacher, for at Chartres the study of sciences other than that of Abelard's choice was preferred. The Chartres school became the centre of twelfth-century humanism, the study of classical literature, and particularly for the study of the natural sciences.

In Paris, the new arrival's sharp intelligence and quick aptitude soon won the attention of the master, but it was not long before they fell out. We have only Abelard's account of the matter, but if we compare this with the conclusion that can be reached on the basis of his other writings it is not difficult to imagine what happened. It is clear that such a gifted pupil was certain to please William, but his enthusiasm soon cooled when it appeared that the young disciple was quite lacking in modesty or in respect towards his teacher when the latter put forward points of view that Abelard believed he could refute. Abelard was taken up with the subject, passionately engaged with the work, and showed no consideration. William's pleasure in his talents therefore rapidly turned to wrath at his impudence. The mature man with the respected name became indignant with the greenhorn who behaved as if he were his equal. Apart from this, Abelard's fellow disciples, many of whom were much older than he, shared their teacher's anger; he directly ignored their precedence in age and years of study in his attempts to be a match for their master. What was particularly wrong of course was that he often succeeded in this! In defeating the teacher he trampled on the disciples: 'This was the beginning of my misfortunes, which are still pursuing me; the more my reputation spread, the more others were inflamed with envy against me.[5] This assessment of the situation during his first period in Paris is probably not completely incorrect, but it must be added that Abelard would scarcely have made the slightest effort to soften William's defeat and thereby lessen the feeling of inferiority among his fellow disciples. Without doubt he was quite intolerable in his distinct awareness of his own superiority. By his behaviour, he gave aversion, already aroused by his mere ability, an appearance of justification; for William and his disciples, virtuous indignation at his blind arrogance could hide the burden of their own envy. It differed very little from the many instances of a similar kind of which Abelard's life was so full. Although his arrogance was perhaps broken by his many misfortunes, he continued by nature and ability to be eager for the fight in the sure certainty that he possessed weapons which made verbal combat a pleasure, and of course there was no decrease in the dislike of him when others realized that he was guilty of no self-deception.

The position at William's school became intolerable; perhaps also Abelard felt that he was wasting his time. In any event, he now wished to put himself forward as a teacher. The only question was, where should he establish his school. He chose Melun, from whence he soon moved to Corbeil which was nearer Paris. He writes that William did everything in his power to prevent his setting up his own school, and was particularly insistent that it should not be near Paris. Abelard sees this as no more than a manifestation of envy, but it is also possible that William considered it his duty to prevent a young disciple, whose education according to the contemporary standard was far from finished, from appearing as an independent master. We have of course no possibility of assessing the feelings that motivated William, but they may not have been as wicked as Abelard wished to make them appear. William may have been envious, but Abelard was, to say the least, vindictive: 'From the outset of my activity in this school I began to win such a name as a dialectician that the reputation not only of my fellow pupils but also of my teacher faded little by little. The result was that I gained even more self-confidence, and as quickly as possible I moved my school to the town of Corbeil, this town being nearer Paris, to be able to deliver from there more frequent and violent dialectical attacks against the enemy.'[6] We have no reason to doubt the account of his rapidly growing reputation, but at the same time Abelard clearly shows that he now desired the total ruin of William. One can hardly blame William for trying to delay the accomplishment of this plan.

Meanwhile, William soon acquired an unexpected ally in Abelard's delicate health. The sojourn at Corbeil had not lasted long before over-exertion forced Abelard to close the school and to return home to his family, where he remained for several years. When in 1108 he appeared in Paris once again William had left his office at Notre Dame; he had founded an institution for regular canons and had himself taken vows. He had not however given up his studies; in the new monastery, St Victor, he continued his public lectures. Abelard says – without directly subscribing to this opinion – that 'it was said that William's decision to change his way of life was the result of ambition, since he hoped in this way to find it easier to obtain a bishopric, whereas his vocation for monastic life is said to have been questionable.' Although Abelard cautiously avoids saying this himself, the intention is obvious enough. Whatever the truth of this, William certainly founded a school at St Victor whose importance was soon to increase by reason of its greatest name: Hugh of St Victor.

Abelard now began once again to listen to William's lectures, this time on the subject of rhetoric. As might be expected, they were soon in conflict with one another. Indeed, it is tempting to believe that Abelard attended not in the expectation of learning but merely to find new opportunities to demonstrate his superiority in discussion with the master. If this was his intention, he fully succeeded. If earlier he had shaken William's confidence, he now rendered his position as a teacher impossible. He forced William to give up his former conception of universals, as a consequence of which William's pupils, in contempt for their teacher, began to gather around Abelard. It is appropriate here to make some reference to the basic facts of this dispute.

In the autobiography, the result of the dispute is referred to with a certain amount of surprise. Abelard recounts that, after

William had been forced to abandon his opinion on universals, he was scarcely 'permitted to teach dialectic any longer; just as if the whole subject rested solely upon this proposition of universals.'[7] In spite of his condescending evaluation of William, Abelard appears to have considered this reaction unreasonable; dialectic was much more than the concept of universals. The basis of the disparity between William and Abelard may be accurately observed in their widely different conception of the meaning of dialectical investigation. Not for nothing had Abelard been taught by the famous Roscelin, although later he sought to dissociate himself from him. Dialectic to Abelard was on the one hand the science of distinguishing between valid and invalid arguments, and on the other of finding one's way to the arguments themselves. Consequently, the dialectician is not concerned with the *things* of this world but with the words by which we indicate these things. Logic is therefore the science of words; that is to say, linguistic logic. Consequently its primary task is to examine what we mean by our concepts in so far as we express them in words. It is then a matter of carrying out the necessary grammatical examination to discover what words and statements mean in the widely different connections in which they can be used. To occupy oneself with things is, to Abelard, to practise not logic but physics. This did not necessarily mean – indeed for his part he had no such intention – that he was sceptical of the validity of our understanding of *things*, but he simply wished to keep the individual disciplines sharply distinct. There were however others, and among them William, who had an entirely different conception. To them, logic was also concerned with things, although in a linguistic form. These 'realists' did not distinguish in the same manner between things outside consciousness and the linguistic expression of the understanding of them. From this difference, which asserted itself in relation to all questions of logic, there now sprang the dispute concerning the reality of universals.

Do the universals we make use of, for example 'man', 'animal', 'flower', correspond to realities outside awareness in the way that these terms in themselves are outside awareness, quite distinct from the individually existent things that comprise them, or is this a matter merely of words by which we summarize the conclusive similarities in a number of independent, existent individuals? This problem was taken over from Antiquity by the philosophy of the Middle Ages, and it gave cause for endless dispute. The strife between William and Abelard already referred to was concerned with this. William was an advocate of the so-called 'naïve realism' which recognized the reality of universals above and independent of the individuals falling within them. By means of his Aristotelian dialectic, Abelard put him in his place to such effect that he was forced to admit defeat. It is easy to understand, bearing in mind the importance of the question at that time, that this cost him his prestige in the intellectual world of Paris. The remark referred to above – 'just as if the whole subject rested solely upon this proposition of universals' – shows that Abelard clearly realized that this was merely a question of detail.

This victory led to an enormous triumph. The new master who succeeded William at the Paris schools now voluntarily withdrew and handed over his position to Abelard, seating himself beneath his lectern. This pleasure was short-lived however as William contrived the dismissal of his successor and his replacement by another, who was of course under no commitment to leave the teaching to Abelard. There was nothing left for Abelard to do but to leave Paris. For a short time he ran a school once more at Melun, but when he learned that William had left Paris he soon returned. This time he settled a little outside the city at the monastery on Mont Ste Geneviève. He does not conceal in his autobiography his intention in this. 'I returned to Paris from Melun immediately in the hope that he (i.e. William) would hereafter leave me in peace. But as I have said, he had caused my position to be occupied by my rival, so I set up camp with my school outside the city on the Mount of the Holy Geneviève in order to, so to say, besiege this man who had taken possession of my place.'[8] It was therefore Abelard's intention by his presence to make the position of William's successor impossible. He recounts that William now returned to come to the rescue of his protégé, but that he only succeeded in damaging him so much that he lost his remaining pupils and was forced to discontinue teaching. Abelard refrains from describing in more detail his and his disciples' struggles during this phase, but proudly refers to what everyone knows! William was now completely ruined from an intellectual viewpoint, and Abelard was left with no significant rival. To all appearances it was now time to reap the fruits of victory. He was then suddenly called to his home.

The event that caused him to return home was quite ordinary at that time. After the children had grown up, the parents had decided to dissolve their home and to take vows. Berengar had already entered a monastery, and Lucia now wished to say farewell to her eldest son before she followed his example. We have no information about his conversations with his mother, but on his return Abelard discontinued his teaching in Paris. Meanwhile, William had become Bishop of Chalôns, to which Abelard refers as some kind of reason for his now wishing to include theology in his studies. It is difficult to see any direct connection between William's appointment and this decision. Had he in mind that he might hope for future peace by also setting up as a teacher of theology, or had this subject become 'available' through William's departure? We do not know. It has been suggested that his mother's influence is a possibility, and this may well be true. It would be quite reasonable for her, on the threshold of the nunnery, to admonish her son to study the knowledge of salvation.

Whatever may be the background, Abelard left for Laon to hear the famous Anselm (c. 1050–1117), the greatest name of the period in theology. Recent research has fully confirmed his reputation and the consequent spread of his school.[9] His attitude was distinctly conservative, strongly bound up with the Fathers, and in his treatment of dogma not very systematic, in that he discussed the various problems within the biblical, historical framework. Dialectic played a very limited role in his theology. It is not surprising that Abelard was disappointed, a fact that he in no way concealed. 'I therefore made my way to this old man who had made his name more through his long years of activity than by intelligence and memory.'[10] As may be seen, Abelard was no advocate of the seniority principle so favoured today! His further description of Anselm's teaching points clearly to what Anselm lacked. The suggestion is that he was very good for those who listened to him, as his volubility was wonderful, but that he was impossible for those who put questions to him, and his words lacked foundation. In other words: hollow eloquence and unfounded assertions. This was of no value to an already practised dialectician. 'When he lit his fire, he filled his house with smoke, but did not drive out darkness with light. His tree, completely covered in leaves as it was, looked beautiful when one viewed it from a distance, but as one drew nearer and saw it more closely it was found to be barren.'[11] From a historical viewpoint this judgment is undoubtedly unjust, but it is of course impossible to expect Abelard to adopt such an attitude. He looked at the matter on the basis of his own opinions on the pursuit of theological study, and by this standard the convincing effect of Anselm's lectures was bound to have been small.

We are prepared to believe Abelard therefore when he continues by saying that he did not lie 'inactive in the shadow of this tree' for many days. In other words he did not very often attend the lectures. Quite naturally his absence was taken as an expression of contempt for the master and therefore resented by the latter's disciples, who stirred up their teacher against him. It eventually came to a showdown between these disciples and Abelard, and this had considerable consequences. They succeeded in so far provoking him that he asserted that he could not conceive what need intelligent people had of aids to an understanding of the Bible, other than Holy Writ itself and the interpretations of the Fathers. This statement was of course strongly provocative for those students who had for years sat beneath Anselm's lectern. They therefore mockingly asked him whether he considered himself to be capable of interpreting the scriptures. To this he readily answered in the affirmative and invited them to a lecture on the following day. As a subject, he chose a difficult text from the Prophet Ezekiel. Some of them had misgivings and advised him to wait a few days, since he was quite unpractised. This Abelard rejected with yet another provocative reply. 'I answered him indignantly that it was not my habit to make progress through diligence but through genius; and I added that I would either withdraw completely or they must attend my lecture without procrastination, as I had directed.'[12] Abelard then recounts that only a few arrived, as most of them considered it ridiculous that he – inexperienced as he still was in theology – ventured to lecture so soon. Those present however found so much pleasure in the lecture that they invited him to continue along the same lines, and students now commenced to flood in.

This episode is certainly enlightening in many aspects. We can to some extent understand how provoking Abelard must have been to his contemporaries. His arrogant behaviour alone doubtless made him many enemies. He certainly cannot have been a pleasant opponent. But the episode also gives us a good insight into his views on scholarship. First, his rejection of the 'seniority viewpoint' goes hand in hand with a firm conviction that nobody makes headway without an accurate knowledge of dialectic. Secondly, it is associated with an equally firm conviction that such knowledge cannot be acquired by all the effort imaginable, but is entirely dependent upon inborn ability. This does not mean that Abelard intermixes dialectic and theology; he is quite aware that the two disciplines have different objects. Dialectic, however, is a tool used to work upon a given text, whatever its nature may be. Later, as we shall see, there was an opportunity for Abelard to elaborate in more detail his point of view on the relationship between dialectic and theology, but the episode here referred to had already given him a clear conception of this.

The students' enthusiasm over his lectures on Ezekiel was not shared by Anselm and his closest disciples, among whom were two men, Alberic of Rheims and Lotulf of Novara, who later had an opportunity to revenge themselves upon Abelard. He believed it was these two men who incited the old master to take action against his young rival. Anselm now forbade Abelard to teach in Laon, on the grounds that he was responsible for all teaching in the town and did not care to take the blame if young Abelard should be guilty of error. Although the organization of studies at this period contains many uncertain points, the intervention of both William and Anselm against Abelard seems to prove that the master had a certain jurisdiction, with responsibility to the local bishop. It was therefore Anselm's right to forbid Abelard to conduct lectures. Later the conditions were such that the leader of studies, *magister scholarum*, formally distributed the right to teach, *licentia docendi*. This was a step towards the conditions in the universities of later periods. But although at the beginning of the century there was as yet no question of fixed legal rules, the master was apparently able to exercise a certain authority.[13]

There was nothing left for Abelard to do but to leave the town. He went to Paris where he was soon appointed *magister scholarum* at Notre Dame. At last he had obtained the position he had for so long desired. He himself says of this: 'A few days later I returned to Paris, and for some years I was in undisturbed possession of the school that had already long ago been intended for me and offered to me, and from which I was at first turned away.'[14] To become *magister scholarum* at Notre Dame meant that Abelard was now adopted into the Chapter as a canon. The important point about this is that he was allotted a prebend from Notre Dame. As master of the school he was consequently rewarded by a share in the property of the cathedral. But this did not involve his ordination. The demarcation between laymen and clergy was of an altogether different kind from that normally imagined on the basis of present-day circumstances. There was no question of Abelard's position becoming basically different as a result of his appointment as master. He had in fact been a 'clerk', *clericus*, from the first day of his studies. It is characteristic that *clerici* and *scholares* are synonymns; both words refer to students. Studying meant that one was automatically included in the clerical system irrespective of whether one had taken holy orders or not. It is worth noting that this was so, irrespective of the science one studied. The schools were and remained Church institutions and therefore subject to the local Church authority. As a consequence of this, masters and students all wore clerical habits and were tonsured.[15]

At the time of William of Champeaux, Paris was famous for its dialectical teaching. It is clear that this fame did not diminish when his victor took over control. But to this subject Abelard now added theology, setting himself immediately to the task of continuing and completing the lectures on Ezekiel he had started. Anselm of Laon suffered great injury from the clash with Abelard, and he died soon afterwards. Only one person could take over his position within theology – the master of the

Paris school. Paris therefore became the place where people gathered from the whole civilized world to study philosophy and theology. During these years, Paris established its leading position to such a degree that the city's central standing was indisputable for centuries to come. The flow of students burst all bounds to begin with, but this prepared the ground for the organization of academic life to such an extent that it was natural for the first fully developed university north of the Alps to be situated in Paris. There is no doubt whatever that more credit for this must be given to Abelard than to any other individual. From this period and later there is abundant proof of his fame and of the unprecedented fascination he evoked among his listeners. This evidence is so unanimous that one must accept that his teaching, in elegance and fertility, surpassed anything previously encountered.

But Abelard was not destined to enjoy his reputation in peace. The struggle to reach the position for which he rightly considered himself qualified was finished, and so was the incentive that had brought him to his goal. About this, he himself says: 'But luck always makes fools conceited; worldly security slackens the power of the intellect and easily destroys it through the temptations of the flesh: I already considered myself the only philosopher left in the world, and no longer feared to be troubled by anyone. I then began to slacken the reins of lust, whereas I had previously lived outwardly continent.'[16] Arrogance and satiety transported him; because of the lack of talented opposition he began to become bored with his success and sought new battlefields. His liaison with Heloïse cured him of boredom but also deprived him of what had been its cause: the lucrative and respected position of *magister scholarum* at Notre Dame.

CHAPTER 3
Heloïse

When Abelard published his autobiography, which includes an account of his love affair with Heloïse, it came into her hands. This led to a correspondence between them, part of which is preserved. Heloïse comments in this correspondence on Abelard's narrative, and there developed a discussion exceedingly valuable in reaching an understanding of their relationship. On the basis of this material it is fairly easy to follow the main points in the course of events, but this is not to say that everything becomes as clear as day. In a matter such as this, there can of course be no real understanding unless the motivation behind the various incidents is known, and this is considerably more difficult. When Abelard wrote his account he had been a monk for many years, and it must be assumed that his view of the events had become coloured by his later circumstances, although there can be no doubt of his desire to be truthful. The correspondence also took place at a period when Abelard and Heloïse had not seen each other for many years. Other than this we have no real sources. The small amount of information we can obtain from elsewhere adds nothing, beyond confirming a few details. We have therefore only the two persons' memories and their discussion of what occurred twelve or thirteen years previously. The task of reaching an understanding by this means must necessarily take in a good deal of uncertainty. But in addition to this, these memories are strongly imbued with concepts on the subject of love that can produce a very strange effect when looked at from a modern viewpoint. Finally it may be relevant to point to the complicating factor: that we are concerned with two people of unusual calibre. Setting aside the necessary technical proficiency, all attempts to understand history are of course conditioned by the worldly experience and imagination of the person seeking to understand. We cannot comprehend more of history than our intelligence and perception allow, and similarly we can do so only within our own environment. But this trivial fact fills one with misgiving when faced with an exceptional character, for who has the intelligence and perception to understand him? But we must dare to make the attempt because Abelard's relationship with Heloïse was so significant in his life that it is impossible to evade it. It is hoped that we shall succeed at least in suggesting what was involved. In the course of this, it may perhaps become clear that this love story throws light upon some important features of the intellectual life of the period.

According to Abelard, it all began as a simple story of seduction. Heloïse does not contradict him on this point, but it is nevertheless difficult completely to accept Abelard's account. We read in the last chapter his comment: that success and prosperity had made him arrogant and had aroused his desire for new conquests. He found a suitable subject in the young Heloïse, Canon Fulbert's niece. She was not only pretty to look at, but she also possessed sufficient breeding and scholarship to suggest that she would value the learned and renowned master as he deserved! It only remained to find a way to establish contact with her, as Abelard had not one moment's doubt that she – or anyone else to whom he might show favour – would yield to his wishes immediately. Described in this way, he appears to have looked upon the whole matter with cynical calculation. In the first place there was 'lust', and thereafter the problem was to find a suitable subject; Heloïse seemed to meet the requirement, as she combined female grace with intelligence and great knowledge. It is, of course, impossible to question the accuracy of this account of the circumstances, but unconsciously Abelard himself denies it a few lines later: '*Completely alight with love* for this young maiden, I therefore sought an opportunity to win her confidence. . . .'[1] It therefore appears that, from the beginning, he was not quite so calculating; or rather, his calculation did not start out from a conscious general desire which then found an objective in Heloïse. Calculation stepped in when Heloïse had aroused his desire, and all that remained was to find a way to win her. But with this modification it is certainly correct that Abelard made his entrance as a seducer.

His calculations were realized in all aspects. Under the pretext that his studies made it difficult for him to do his own housekeeping, he suggested to Heloïse's uncle that he be allowed to take his meals in his house in return for suitable payment. The uncle, who according to Abelard was completely dominated by two passions, avarice and a burning love for his niece, saw in this an opportunity to take advantage of Abelard's learning. He therefore not only agreed to the proposal but in fact *asked* Abelard to move into his house on condition that he attended to Heloïse's education in his spare time. She was entrusted completely to his care, with a right to punish her if she were negligent in her studies. Abelard believes that this credulity, which in his opinion was as startling as if Fulbert had left a newborn lamb in the care of a hungry wolf, had two grounds – love for the girl and Abelard's own reputation until then of continence. He did not delay in making use of the opportunity, and everything points to the fact that Heloïse gave herself to him without hesitation. 'Under the pretence of lessons we abandoned ourselves to our love undisturbed, and that solitude, far from the eyes of others, coveted by passion was made easy for us because of the studies. Consequently, when we had opened our books, more words of love appeared than of reading; kisses were more numerous than sentences. More often hands found their way to her bosom than to the books; more frequently did love cause our eyes to meet than did study direct them towards the writing in the book. To arouse less suspicion, I beat her now and then, not in hot temper but in love, not in anger but in tenderness, and this beating surpassed all balms in sweetness. In short, we left no phase of love untried in our passion, and if love-making could find the unusual, we tried this also. And the less experience we had in these joys, the greater was our burning ardour in abandoning ourselves to them, and the less did we feel fatigue.'[2] It is evident that there were lively goings-on when the respected philosopher and theologian, with nature and perhaps Ovid (Gilson's expression) as his teacher, experimented with his pretty and talented private pupil!

But during all this something happened that Abelard could not have foreseen. Heloïse became much more to him than a diversion. When the planned goal had been reached Abelard lost control of events. From now on he thought only of her and was occupied only with his love. Within a very short time he let go by default everything he had fought for and achieved by so much effort. He leaves us in no doubt in the correspondence of the extent to which he was ruled by his desire: 'I was bound to you with such a burning desire that I preferred these – pleasures – to both God and myself.'[3] He reminds Heloïse with horror that, in his passion, he was unable, even in awe of God, to restrain himself even during the festivals of the Church. Heloïse on the other hand had misgivings, but gave in to his threats and lashings as he says.[4] To understand correctly the importance of this, we must remember that we are concerned with a man for whom there was no shadow of doubt that Almighty God saw and condemned his actions. In short, he was staking his eternal salvation. He *knew* this, but in spite of it was unable to act differently. We may question the quality and nature of his love of her, as indeed both he and Heloïse do in their correspondence, but not its intensity.

He preferred Heloïse not only to God but to himself. But did he perhaps mean that he preferred – in his own words – 'these pleasures'? The violent activity under the pretence of home-teaching made it impossible for him to do justice to himself when he was lecturing. As he himself quite rightly says, it takes great effort to stay awake at night to cultivate love and then to attend to studies during the day. It was impossible for him to drum up any special interest for philosophy and theology. With the preoccupation of a sleepwalker, he spoke from memory. The disciples of course could not help noticing his lack of inspiration, and it was therefore not long before they knew the reason. Abelard, who until then had lived for scholarship and the unique position it had given him in the world of learning, now watched with indifference as all he had won withered away. He rightly says that he preferred his love to himself, for it was his former image of himself that he relinquished. And yet in this he showed himself to be precisely the personality he in fact was. What more could one wish for by way of individuality? It is well known that Burckhardt considered this very individualism to be characteristic of the Renaissance when contrasted with the Middle Ages. 'The discovery of man' must have meant that the individual saw himself as the point of orientation in existence, so to say, whereas in the Middle Ages man looked upon himself collectively in relation to God. Abelard is an awkward dissonance in the harmony of this conception. Which demands more 'individuality'; to idolize oneself in a godless universe or to go one's way to the end in the full knowledge that one is damned by God?

Although in his public activities Abelard was now nothing more than 'a reciter of old ideas', love gave him an inspiration that brought him new fame in which Heloïse shared: he became a poet. Unfortunately we know nothing more of these love songs than what Heloïse and Abelard have to say of them. The poems themselves have disappeared. In his autobiography Abelard refers to them in passing, but because of their wide dissemination he considers it unnecessary, even at that time, to refer to them in more detail. 'Most of these poems, as you well know, are still widely known and are sung in many districts, particularly by people who take pleasure in life in a similar way.'[5] Some of Heloïse's remarks are rather more informative. It appears that Abelard not only wrote the poems but also set them to music. A remark – that even the unlettered could not avoid remembering Abelard because of the sweet sound of his music – suggests that they were written in Latin.[6] Heloïse was of course the subject of the songs. 'All streets, every house, echoed with my name,'[7] she writes. Sitting in her cloister cell she recalls their impact with obvious delight. 'This in particular was why women sighed for your love. And because the greater part of these poems praised our love they made me known within a short time in many districts, and inflamed many women with envy towards me.'[8] We may assume that Heloïse exaggerates a little, but the many proofs of the attraction Abelard's personality exercised upon his contemporaries make it credible that this fascination, mixed with some virtuous indignation, did in fact make him a favourite

with the women and Heloïse the object of their envy. It must
not be forgotten that this kind of poetry was something of an
innovation in these regions. We have no other evidence of love
poems from northern France as early as this, which makes it
doubly regrettable that this section of Abelard's poetry has been
lost.

It is understandable that the famous philosopher's love not
only aroused reciprocal emotions in the young girl but also
caused her to feel favoured before all others. She indeed
possessed, as Abelard had correctly foreseen, the qualities necessary to appreciate his greatness. Even before she came to know
Abelard she was admired throughout the country for her
scholarship.[9] But this was nothing compared with the fame that
now became hers. Within a short time, of course, everyone in
Paris and many outside the city knew what was happening in
Fulbert's house; only the master of the house was still in ignorance. Abelard recounts that kindly people informed him, but
that he was unwilling to believe it. At last the truth dawned
upon him for, as Abelard says, 'What all can grasp in the hand
cannot easily remain hidden from one individual.'[10] We do not
know how long it was before Fulbert found out – only that it
happened 'after the passage of several months'. Nor are we
informed how the discovery came about. The scandal naturally
resulted in Abelard's having to move out. Despair and shame
filled the lovers, while Fulbert's rage knew no bounds. It was
now to be proved in earnest that this was no casual or trivial
affair. One result of the exposure was that the lovers now
realized the depth of their love. Abelard writes of this: 'When
the agony of shame was past, we became less sensitive to feelings
of shame. Indeed, as the agony of shame became less, the more
naturally did the exercise of our love come to us.'[11] The result of
the discovery was therefore that they now openly confirmed
what everyone knew. They wrote to one another during the
separation, and eventually Heloïse told him that she was preg-
nant. She asked Abelard to decide what they should do in this
situation. It is characteristic of Heloïse that in spite of the difficult circumstances the expected child made her 'radiantly
happy'. Abelard does not say what his emotions were at this
news; however, he immediately decided upon the action to take.

By arrangement with Heloïse he abducted her from her uncle's house while the latter was away and took her disguised as a nun to his sister in Brittany. Here she remained until the confinement was over. She had a boy, to whom she gave the name, Astrolabius. We may readily believe that Fulbert was beside himself with indignation. His house had been disgraced by the events, and if we are to believe Abelard – and there is no reason not to do so – he was thereafter constantly occupied with thoughts of how he could take his revenge. But as Heloïse was living with Abelard's family it was difficult for him to act. Abelard of course felt ill at ease with such a threat hanging over his head, for this was what Fulbert's hatred and vindictiveness amounted to, and he now tried to ease the situation. He went to see Fulbert, admitted that he had betrayed him in the most shameful manner and offered to compensate him. This compensation was to consist in his marrying Heloïse, but secretly so that his reputation should not suffer! He recounts that Fulbert agreed to this, and he now believed that everything was set to rights.

But this was by no means the case. In the first place, Heloïse was definitely against the plan, although she gave in to Abelard's dogged persistence in his wish to marry her. Secondly, a *secret* marriage was by no means sufficient compensation for Fulbert, whose disgrace was *public*. Abelard had his way; he brought Heloïse back to Paris and there they were married early one morning in the presence of Fulbert and a few friends. Heloïse then returned to her uncle's house as if nothing had happened and Abelard resumed his teaching. But the situation was quite intolerable. Fulbert could not forget what had happened to him and immediately broadcast far and wide that his niece was now married to Abelard. He now however had to suffer the indignity that Heloïse, to protect Abelard, swore this was not true. Fulbert's impotence against Abelard now caused him to give vent to his anger on Heloïse. It became obvious that she could not remain in her uncle's house, and Abelard abducted her a second time. He did not, as might be expected, take her back to his sister in Brittany, where they had left their son, but to the convent of Argenteuil near Paris where Heloïse had been educated.

It was this action that decided their fate. Heloïse's family now assumed – it is impossible to say whether rightly or not – that Abelard intended to rid himself of her by causing her to take the veil. There is confirmation of this in the fact that Heloïse, following Abelard's wishes, put on the habit – which was in no way a condition for residing at the convent. Fulbert and his relations then prepared the cruel plan they soon succeeded in carrying out. They bribed Abelard's servant to open the door of his house during the night, took the sleeping man by surprise and castrated him. Overcome by shame, Abelard sought refuge in the monastery of St Denis, first having commanded Heloïse to take the veil.

Heloïse later asserted that the marriage was the cause of their ill-fortune, and that she had foreseen this before it took place. Abelard writes that Heloïse, when she realized that she could not make him change his mind, concluded the dialogue with the following words: 'Now only one thing remains; that we shall be destroyed, and that there will follow no less pain than there was love before.' He adds: 'Nor were these words bereft of prophesy, as all the world has had cause to admit.'[12] The connection certainly seems to be quite clear: marriage – Fulbert's publication of it – Heloïse's denial – Fulbert's rage towards her – the flight to Argenteuil – the crime against Abelard – the necessity of a separation. What is far more important than establishing this, however, is that the marriage itself and the attitude of the two people towards it throws a clear light upon their relationship. To begin at the least significant point, it is quite apparent that they were not in agreement as to the effect of the marriage upon Fulbert; Abelard assumed that it would have the intended reconciliatory effect upon him, but Heloïse who knew him better did not believe for one moment that he could forget his disgrace. But the difference went far deeper, as it was based more upon the impulse of the heart than upon the premeditation of the intellect. Abelard reveals what was probably his true reason for desiring a marriage in his second letter to Heloïse, where he writes: 'God had bound us to one another by the indissoluble pact of the marriage sacrament, while I wished to keep for myself for ever what I loved beyond all reason.'[13] On grounds that we shall discuss in a moment, Abelard was anxious to have the public believe him to be unmarried. If nevertheless he desired a marriage, it was so to say out of jealousy towards Heloïse's future; by marrying her he bound her in such a manner that neither she nor her family would ever be able to push him aside, for example by another marriage. But by enforcing a marriage and at the same time demanding that it remain a secret he denied her the right to whatever she might have enjoyed by marriage to a young man – a respected and honourable position in society. We may be tempted to dismiss his attitude as highly selfish, but if we are in any way to understand him we must bear in mind that the consequences were such that there must have been *very* substantial reasons for desiring secrecy. Were there such reasons?

When we put this question it comes to light that the only plausible answer, which Etienne Gilson has painstakingly explored in his book on Heloïse and Abelard, leads us directly into processes of thought closely bound up with the 'twelfth-century Renaissance'. Apart from this, the question also has a direct connection with Heloïse's reluctance to enter into matrimony. Abelard recounts that she was against the plan for two reasons: the danger he thereby exposed himself to and the disgrace. The danger she considered to be her uncle's vindictiveness, which she knew would not abate. But what had she in mind when she said it would be a disgrace for Abelard? He had not at that time become ordained, and in spite of his position as a canon there was no reason whatever why he should not marry. It is of course true that in so doing he excluded himself from later becoming a priest, and perhaps – like so many masters before him – reaching very high office within the Church. This he no doubt realized, and *this* therefore is the sacrifice he was prepared to make for his passion. It is difficult to be sure whether he could have remained a canon, and although there appears to have been no canonical obstacle, a married *magister scholarum* at Notre Dame would have been quite exceptional. But whatever were the facts of this matter, it could in any case have had nothing to do with *keeping secret* the marriage. The subsequent events interrupted his career to such a degree that we cannot be certain on these matters. It can only be said that if marriage meant renouncing one or another of his dignities, then so did a secret marriage. Any suggestion that the 'disgrace' was associated with something directly unlawful is out of the question.

But in his extensive account of Heloïse's to some extent very learned objections he leads us in quite another direction. Briefly, this is as follows: entry into marriage is at variance with the classical philosophical ideal to which Heloïse and Abelard both deferred in their common admiration of Abelard! He himself formulates this very clearly in the introduction to his account of the abduction, '... it is certainly true that the philosophers – quite apart from the holy men, that is to say those who give heed to the admonitions of Holy Writ – could attribute most of the credit for the *respect* they enjoyed to their *perfect contin-ence*'.[14] It is the very argument put forward by Heloïse. She first draws his attention to Paul, but if Abelard is unwilling to accept the exhortations of the Apostle or of the holy men, she asks him to take notice of what the philosophers have written on this subject. St Jerome supplies her with several excellent examples to illustrate the inconsistency between marriage and philo-sophical studies. She herself describes with great eloquence the incompatible contrast between philosophical study and domestic chores and worries: 'Finally, is it possible for he who is immersed in religious or philosophical reflections to tolerate the crying of children, the crooning of nurses when they quieten them and the noisy bustle of men and women servants? Moreover, can anyone tolerate the constant uncleanliness of small children?'[15] Heloïse anticipates the objection – that the rich can – with the reply that philosophers are not in this position. She concludes with a quotation from Seneca: 'There is little difference between giving up philosophy and pursuing it in the face of interrup-tions. For if the pursuit of it is interrupted, it is finished.'[16] To give Abelard proper warning, she adds that if pagans could live in this way, how much more should he, a cleric and a canon, fight against being devoured by 'shameful lust'. But she is pre-pared to abandon the special appeal to him as a cleric. If he has no concern for what he owes to God, he should at least defend his dignity as a philosopher.

Heloïse uses every lever she can find. Arguments of Christian asceticism and pagan philosophy rub shoulders, but it is first and foremost a matter that concerns Abelard the *philosopher*. She

thinks also of his possible future in the Church: '... imagine
the loss to the Church that will follow such a marriage.'[17]
Nevertheless, it is clear that she wishes to uphold a way of life
independent in principle of Christianity and the Church;
Abelard's 'disgrace' lies in his renouncing this. It is likewise
clear that Abelard shared this ideal in every respect. The disagreement between them is not ideological but personal, because
it is concerned with the different quality of their love. The
reasons that Heloïse puts forward *against* their marriage are just
the same as those which make him wish it to be *kept secret!*
From this we can draw some conclusions, on the one hand
concerning their relationship and on the other concerning their
differing demands upon Abelard personally.

Perhaps we can express the difference between their attitudes
by remembering that Abelard is concerned with the pursuit of
two aims, which strictly speaking are incompatible; both concern himself, Heloïse coming into the picture only as the object
of *his* aspirations. Heloïse on the other hand has only one goal.
The fulfilment of her love subsists only in Abelard's glory; for
this reason she herself withdraws. Abelard wishes to live up to
the philosophical ideal but his jealous attitude towards other
eventualities makes him also wish to secure Heloïse for himself.
The result is therefore the unhappy idea of a secret marriage.
Heloïse is concerned for Abelard's honour because in this only is
her own love consummated. This can be attained only if he is
truly and not merely *apparently* living in accordance with the
philosophical ideal. In betraying the ideal – and thereby himself
– by being sensually tied to Heloïse he betrays their love and
consequently betrays her, for the purpose of her life is him and
him alone. Seen in this light, the two parties' demands upon
Abelard are therefore determined by their very relationship. To
be able to satisfy the needs of his selfish 'possessive' love for
Heloïse, Abelard pushes aside his demands upon himself. But to
retain the purity of her love, Heloïse must assert her demands
upon Abelard even to her own cost. Self-assertion, although of a
very subtle nature, may also be detected here; Heloïse can only
be true to herself by sacrificing herself to Abelard's glory as a
philosopher. When he demands that she should marry him she
does so in spite of all her objections, and in so doing she as it

were withdraws herself on to a new plane for his sake. She now 'sacrifices her sacrifice' because it is impossible for her to go against him.

This conception of love, to which Heloïse gives expression and moreover on which she is prepared to act, she undoubtedly shared with Abelard. But he was unable to live up to it. 'Renaissance' also enters into the picture here. Like many other people in the twelfth century, the couple were inspired by Cicero's treatise 'On friendship' (De amicitia) which describes 'disinterested love' as the only worthy expression of true friendship. It is apparent from Heloïse's letter that there is no trace whatever of a religious motive in her will to sacrifice her life's happiness for the sake of Abelard's 'honour'. During their cohabitation, the atmosphere of the relationship between the two 'philosophers' had been conditioned by Cicero's ideas. The circumstance that the relationship was also erotic had altered nothing ideologically.[18] They agree later that Heloïse, because of Abelard's sensuality, sought his pleasure, not her own. That she later found it difficult to forget the pleasure she had herself enjoyed is quite another matter!

When Heloïse sought to prevent the marriage by evoking for Abelard the philosophic ideal to which he himself deferred, she did so with no certainty that he would allow himself to be persuaded in this way. But she had other possibilities – an appeal to that very sensuality which threatened to disgrace him. With courage and maturity surprising in so young a girl she declares that she would far rather be his mistress than his wife. She lures him by stressing that periodical separations would make the pleasures of their association all the sweeter, the more rare they were. But the alternatives of mistress or wife hold more for Heloïse than a last desperate appeal to Abelard. Two points of view come to light here. First, it would be more decorous for him if she continued as his mistress. By this she means that although the liaison is already a betrayal of the philosophic ideal, it is not abandoned for ever as it would be by a marriage. This concession she is therefore prepared to make to him: that for a time he can assuage her demands upon him by continuing the liaison with her. We can easily appreciate that Heloïse, in spite of her high ideals and strong desire to live in accordance with them, reserved to herself this possibility of preserving her happiness, if this could be achieved without taking final leave of these ideals. But from this it becomes clear that the philosophical argument against marriage would lead to an absolute termination of the relationship. This of course was perfectly clear to Heloïse, and there is no reason to doubt that she was ready to face it.

There is however another aspect of Heloïse's preference for her status of mistress. A glimpse of this may be seen in Abelard's account of her reasoning: 'and thus it became tenderness alone that preserved her for me, and not marriage ties holding me fast by force'.[19] She herself brings this out even more clearly in her commentary on the autobiography. In a passage where she stresses the unselfish nature of her love she declares that it had always seemed 'sweeter' to her to be called mistress or paramour, even though the title of wife is *considered* to be something more sacred and more binding. She bases this on the argument that the more she humiliated herself the greater tenderness might she have expected from him, while at the same time, as pointed out above, she thereby 'did less to impair his fame'.[20] But apart from the question of Abelard's honour as a philosopher, Heloïse prefers the 'free' love relationship to marriage. The true reason for this is more apparent from the context of her letter than from any individual statement.

Immediately after this quotation, Heloïse thanks Abelard for not having omitted to mention any of the reasons by which she sought to make him give up the idea of marriage. But she adds that he has suppressed most of the reasons that made her prefer 'love to marriage, freedom to chains'. It might be expected that she would herself follow this by putting forward these reasons, and this she in fact does to some extent. She begins with an apparently somewhat banal observation: If Augustus, the lord of the whole world, wished to marry her and hand over to her power over all the earth for all eternity, she would still consider it a greater honour to be called Abelard's whore than Augustus' Empress. It is tempting to shrug one's shoulders at this with the comment that any little girl in love would probably be prepared to make these words her own. But if one has spent some time in Heloïse's company one becomes more cautious. In any case, the last thing one could call her is banal. It must be allowed that she is not very convincing when, as a reason for her example, she then says that it is neither riches nor power that determine a man's worth, and that the woman who prefers a rich man to a poor man sells herself, because it is his fortune and not the man himself she desires. To find a meaning in this beyond the trivial, one must read on. Heloïse now proceeds to quote a passage she has found in Cicero.[21] The philosophically learned Aspasia is said to have used this argument upon Xenophon and his wife in order to restore the good relationship between them, and she is said to have concluded with the following words: 'From the moment that you come to the realization that there is no better man nor more excellent woman on earth, there can be no obstacle to your recognition and your enjoyment of that happiness which is usually allotted to you – for the one is the husband of the best possible wife and the other the wife of the best possible husband.' Heloïse approves of these words: 'Sacred is this error, blissful is this delusion between man and wife, where perfect love preserves the marriage pact inviolate, not so much through bodily faithfulness as through mental chastity.' But for Heloïse the conclusive point is that the happiness delusion can give to other women had been given to her by truth! She had no need, she says, to *believe* about Abelard what she and all the world *knew*: 'consequently my love for you became the more true, the further it was removed from delusion'.[22] This is later substantiated in more detail by a vivid description of Abelard's fame, favour with women, etc., which it is not necessary to go into here.

What has here been recounted appears to present no direct reason for preferring freedom to 'chains'. The example of Augustus says no more than that Heloïse prefers a free relationship with Abelard to a marriage for the sake of power and riches. In the eyes of Heloïse marriages of this nature are equivalent to prostitution, and one can scarcely disagree with her in this. She later puts forward the concept that a true marriage presupposes 'the blissful delusion', and she continues by stressing the truth of her own love. *She* needed no delusion, for nobody could be compared with Abelard, etc. It must be remembered that Heloïse is not writing to a stranger who is unaware of her manner of thought, and must therefore have everything explained in detail to understand her meaning. She is writing to the man with whom she is intimately associated also on the intellectual plane. If we now connect up some of the points set out in the text, a deep meaning comes to light in these apparently somewhat trite and scattered reflections. First: Heloïse uses marriage for the sake of power or riches as an example, but it is obvious that her conception of love as 'disinterested' presupposes that all marriages in which one of the parties wishes to obtain 'something', that is to say where something other than the actual marriage partner is of importance, must be considered as no more than prostitution. This is apparent from the lines immediately preceding the paragraph referred to: 'Never have I, as God is my witness, sought anything in you other than yourself; it was you and you alone, not yours, that I desired. It was not the marriage pact nor anything one might call a dowry I expected; and finally it was not my own pleasure or will but yours I strove to satisfy, as you well know.'[23] As we can see, here also marriage itself is used as an example. It appears on a parallel with 'dowry' – that is, riches.

Secondly: In contrast to a marriage that may be considered as no more than prostitution, there is mental chastity – the realization that the beloved is 'the best' – which makes it possible for perfect love to keep the marriage pact inviolate. This mental chastity – which is the only criterion – Heloïse possessed because the truth of her love was the most complete imaginable, since she needed no holy delusion to help her regard Abelard as the best. Consequently marriage could *add nothing significant*. This train of thought is strongly sustained by their common ethical principle, which may perhaps be referred to as 'the ethic of the pure intention'. It is expressed briefly and clearly by Heloïse in this way: 'For it is not the accomplishment of the matter but the intention of the one accomplishing it that constitutes the offence; it is not what is done, but the disposition in which it is done that is judged by righteousness.'[24]

Consequently Heloïse was bound to prefer freedom to coercion, as only in freedom was there certainty that mental chastity and pure intention alone governed the relationship. In marriage there was danger that coercion, or 'prostituting' desire for something other than the other person *himself*, would violate the perfection of love. Against this background, Abelard's adherence to his wish for marriage must have been offensive not only in the sense that he thereby brought dishonour and consequent shame upon her, who wished for nothing but him, but it was offensive also in that he affronted her by showing mistrust of her. How could she otherwise interpret his wish? It is true that in the letters she does not reproach him with *this*, but it follows from her way of thought that she must have taken it as a deep offence against 'mental chastity'. As we have seen, such an allegation would certainly have been fully justified.

Not for nothing was Heloïse Abelard's disciple. The concepts determining her view on marriage in general and on her own in particular had come originally from him. But what he, under the pressure of his grudging sentiments, was unable to implement in practice, she made real. In doing so she showed that she was not merely an admiring echo of her beloved but that even in her early youth she possessed an independence that made these concepts her own property. The famous logician on the other hand was unable in practice to defend the ideals of Antiquity that he could postulate in such brilliant formulae. From his earliest youth he had become far too accustomed to having everything revolve around himself, Abelard. The conflict he found himself in was probably to a certain extent the conflict between his vocation and love; not between love of philosophy and of Heloïse, but between love of the image of himself as the greatest philosopher of the period and love of himself as the possessor of Heloïse. The result was the half-measure expressed in the idea of the secret marriage. But if we bear in mind that this compromise was not a bargain struck between two inclinations incomplete in themselves but a struggle between two passions, we become more wary of making a quick judgment upon him. It is characteristic of Abelard the intellectual that everything he undertook throughout his life was impassioned, but it would be wrong to isolate his self-centredness and to argue that this was his only passion. To be sure, it always played a part, but in everything Abelard did it appears that he could do no other than go on to the end, no matter what consequences it had for him. While the liaison with Heloïse was officially secret she was so much the central figure of his life that apparently without hesitation he discarded everything he had won in the world of learning.

Upon the disclosure of the liaison, he awoke from his intoxication and realized that it was necessary to make up his mind. To give up philosophy would have meant to him his destruction as a person. But neither could he give up Heloïse, the one and only creature or object that had ever made him stray from the course he had planned in his youth and had followed with such success. Perhaps it was his human instincts themselves that made it impossible for him to come to any real decision at the moment of truth, and made him, almost against his nature, try to compromise. It cannot be denied or concealed that Heloïse was his superior, but it is perhaps too easy a solution to interpret his behaviour as moral turpitude. Nor should we overlook in this connection the sacrifice involved for an ambitious man to give up any idea of a career in the Church, quite apart from what it must have meant to him to be forced into the position of having Heloïse teach him that he had betrayed the ideals he had believed in, and still believed in.

After the marriage, it was still Heloïse who was forced to bear the burden. Consistent as always, she did what Abelard expected of her after she had given in to his wishes. It is difficult to imagine what it must have cost her to lie when her family began to spread the news of their marriage. But the reputation of her Abelard was at stake and, in spite of personal anguish, there can have been no doubt in her mind of what she was to do. The couple did not of course see much of each other at this period, although Abelard writes that they met now and then in deep secret. We do not know in what manner Fulbert, in his anger at Heloïse's denial of the marriage, harassed her; but at all events it became unbearable for her. Abelard then took her to the convent at Argenteuil, and thereby gave rise to the suspicion that caused her family to take such a cruel revenge upon him.

We are unaware of his intentions in placing Heloïse in the convent. Neither of them say anything on this subject that might form a clue. We must not however disregard the simple possibility that he had no long-term plan at all. Argenteuil was in the neighbourhood of Paris, which may be sufficient explanation for his preferring this to the distant home of his sister.

Abelard could visit her there without interrupting his teaching, and this he certainly did. In one of the letters he reminds Heloïse that once during a visit his uncontrollable passion caused them shamelessly to desecrate the refectory, which was consecrated to the Holy Virgin, as there was no other place for them to go.[25] But it was probably not very long before punishment caught up with him.

The crime became known immediately all over the city, and Abelard asserts that the pity shown him made him suffer more than did the mutilation. In his momentary despair and disgrace he saw his entire fame destroyed, and he could not contemplate ever showing himself again among people. He thought with horror of the harsh words of Old Testament law concerning the aversion eunuchs evoke in the eyes of God. Whether, as he writes, he already at that time saw the events as an expression of God's justice, is perhaps questionable.[26] But we know from other sources that he strove in hate and indignation to bring down punishment upon the culprits. Two of the accomplices, including his servant, were caught and punished in the most horrible manner.[27] But although Abelard may have ante-dated his remorse and, as far as it went, his acceptance of the events as an expression of God's righteous condemnation, he is certainly being accurate when he writes as follows: 'In the miserable state and the crushing despair in which I found myself, it was much more – I admit – overpowering shame than pious penitence that drove me to seek shelter under the mantle of the monasteries. But before that my bride, at my command, took the veil and entered the convent.'[28] Abelard saw no other alternative than to hide himself from people. But he first ensured that Heloïse became a nun in the convent at Argenteuil. He writes that many tried to dissuade her from doing this, but in vain. When Heloïse had taken the vow Abelard himself entered the fashionable Benedictine monastery of St Denis.

Abelard had become a different person. The conflict that had divided him had now been resolved in an unexpected manner. The ties laid upon him by his new existence as a monk were not oppressive; a monastery was not only the sole remaining place for him to live, but it also offered him what he really needed: peace from people. It was quite another matter with Heloïse.

She had not become another person, and she felt no vocation for convent life. She had only one motive – to obey Abelard. He hurt her deeply by letting her be the first to take vows. She saw in this – probably correctly – an expression of distrust, which appears still to have pained her twelve or thirteen years later.[29] She was prepared to follow him, but from the expressions she uses later to remind him of her obedience it is clear that this had not been easy for her: 'passion was transformed into such a madness that it deprived itself of the only thing it yearned for, with no hope of recovering it; for, following your command, I myself immediately changed both clothing and mind in order to demonstrate that you alone possessed both my body and my soul.'[30] In a different place she writes: 'It was your command and not divine love that made me put on the sacred habit.'[31] Faced with a future without him, with no calling and with no hope, she obediently subjected herself to the conditions he commanded her to live under. But it is apparent from the correspondence that it was only her clothing and her outward behaviour she changed and not in any way her mind, whereas for Abelard entry into the monastery really became a 'conversion' in the mediaeval sense of the word: a new life of penance and humility.

This becomes apparent from the way the two persons concerned assess what had occurred. Only at one point are they more or less agreed – in their view of the quality of Abelard's love. They both conclude that it consisted only of sensual desire, and they also agree that it does not deserve the name of love. But at this point agreement ends. When it comes to the criteria for assessing this question, as well as the whole of their relationship and its consequences, they differ widely from one another. For Heloïse the yardstick is still the concept of love that had determined her relationship with Abelard throughout the crisis surrounding the marriage. Abelard on the other hand is conditioned by his new way of life as a monk. Although a detailed analysis of the correspondence is beyond the scope of this account, a reference to some of the notable manifestations of this fundamental disagreement appears desirable at this point, and it will also prove useful in explaining Heloïse's importance in Abelard's destiny.

Heloïse makes no attempt to hide that Abelard is now, as

ever, the person on whom her life depends: 'For you are the only one capable of bringing me sorrow and joy, or of rendering me consolation.'[32] This is not an exaggerated or impulsive statement, and it should be accepted quite literally. Thus writes the nun, highly respected for her exemplary life. If we now ask why it was not possible for her to obtain consolation in God, as might be expected from one in her position, she leaves us in no doubt as to the answer. At the beginning of her first letter she reproaches Abelard for having neglected her for so long. In this she sees evidence that it had been desire rather than love that tied him to her, for he forgot her as soon as what he desired was at an end. She asks him at least to write to her, and then adds: 'It was indeed no pious fear of God that led me, a very young girl, into the hard yoke of convent life, but only and entirely your command; if in this I merit no gratitude at all from you, then judge for yourself how fruitless is my effort! I cannot expect for this any reward from God, since it is indisputable that I have as yet done nothing for love of Him.'[33] In another place she says that in all the circumstances of her life she has been more afraid of going against him than of going against God.[34] It would not be difficult to point to other quotations of the same nature, but this seems unnecessary. It is already clear that, in truth, it is Abelard who is her god. It is love of him and fear of him that guides all her actions, and at his hand she expects – or at least hopes – to receive reward and consolation.

This leads us to the roots of the deep conflict that dominates the life of the thirty-year-old abbess, and which she implores Abelard to help her to solve. She is an advocate of the ethic of pure intention and must therefore condemn her own life. This, to be sure, is outwardly blameless, but it is quite unrelated to true conventual life. This torments her and causes her without hesitation to brand herself a hypocrite. But the simple and readily understood difference between her very earthly love and the divine love towards which a nun should devote all her energy is not a satisfactory illustration of the conflict. To understand the whole range of her suffering we must be clear about two things: first, the background, not only to her taking the veil but also to her wish now to be a nun in the true sense; secondly, we must try to understand what being a nun meant to her. We already know the answer to the first point: she became a nun and genuinely wished to be one because Abelard – her god – had so commanded her. For Heloïse, this command meant not only that she should put on a nun's habit but that she should *be* a nun, because for her it is only the intention that counts and never the outward behaviour. But what does it really mean to be a nun? It means living and acting from love of God. But this is the very concept that is not consistent with 'disinterested' love when it is seen, as Heloïse sees it, as a total commitment. If we bear in mind that Heloïse's unconditional love of Abelard makes him her god, it becomes apparent that the conflict is insoluble. Because the god – Abelard – so commands, Heloïse wishes to serve God; indeed she wishes to do nothing else. But this implies an impossibility as, because it is at the command of Abelard that she wishes it, *God* cannot become God for her. This presupposes that she should give up the concept of total love and, as her assessment of their relationship shows, this she is not willing to do.

It is however true that here and there in her letters opinions can be found that are based upon conventual ethics, but it is nonetheless clear that she has in no way changed. There is only one thing she regrets: that she allowed herself to be persuaded to marry Abelard. She can refer to what went before as 'sin' and she can express a wish to do penance for this, but the voice of her heart is quite different. 'How indeed can it be called doing penance for one's sins, however hard one tortures the body, if the mind still retains the will to sin and burns with the same desire as before.'[35] Heloïse makes no attempt to deceive herself: 'But so sweet to me were the sensual pleasures of the passion we enjoyed together that they cannot arouse my displeasure; indeed they scarcely disappear from my memory. . . . I should certainly groan about what I have done; but I sigh rather over what I have lost.'[36] The thought that the marriage itself was the beginning of all their suffering fills her with bitterness against the God she wishes to serve, as Abelard has commanded her. In particular, she cannot bear to think of the manner by which their separation occurred. In all these misfortunes Abelard is her only consolation, and it appears to her that he has failed. In this she sees evidence that he was formerly bound to her merely by desire. But now he has settled her manner of life once and for all, and she therefore begs him to help her to bear it.

Abelard does not measure his love for Heloïse by the standards they both once recognized and which Heloïse still considers to be the only valid ones. He can therefore accept neither her assessment of the bygone events nor her interpretation of the misfortune that followed therefrom. Only harsh words of denunciation remain to be said by him concerning their relationship before and during the marriage. He does not spare himself, but at the same time stresses that they were both guilty. He therefore gives no sanction to Heloïse's reference to the pure intention. For him the whole relationship was sinful, and the tragic interruption of it he sees as proof that it pleased the divine mercy to deliver them and give them – although involuntarily – an opportunity to win salvation in a life of pious submission. He agrees with her that his own love may be evaluated as no more than desire, but the criterion for this is not disinterested love but love of quite a different kind. In his attempt to rid Heloïse of this bitterness towards God, which as he says not only separates her from God but also from him, he employs her own views on love: 'What does Christ seek in you, I ask, other than you yourself?' He is a true friend Who desires you yourself, not what is yours. He is a true friend Who, when He was about to die for you, said: "Greater love hath no man than this, that a man lay down his life for his friends." He nourished a true love for you, but I did not. My love, which brought sin to us both, should be called desire, not love. I satisfied my pitiful passion on you, and that was all I loved. I have suffered for you, you say, and perhaps this is true, but it was rather through you, and even that was involuntary; it was not for love of you but by compulsion; it brought you not salvation but pain. He on the other hand has suffered for your salvation; He has suffered voluntarily for you, He, Who through His suffering heals all frailty and removes all suffering.'[37]

For Abelard, the love Heloïse has tried to make tangible and has looked for in vain in him is to be found in God alone. When she asks him for help he tries to give her what he has – an urge to seek and find love in Christ. He also believes they are still tied to one another. He shows this, for example, in his plea to Heloïse to arrange for his body to be taken to her convent after his death. But it is a bond of a different nature than before. There is for him no doubt that this bond is far more intense and firm than that which bound them before their 'conversion'. He must therefore rebuke her when she complains about her harsh fate. God in his mercy has saved them from the temptations of the world. But he does not forget that there is a fundamental difference in their circumstances. He is freed once and for all from 'the fires of passion', while she is still plagued by the 'incessant impulses of the flesh'. He sees in this a special divine mercy: 'because he who must always fight can also expect the crown; for only he is crowned "who fights according to law". But I can expect no crown as I have no reason to fight.'[38] Abelard clearly feels that Heloïse is not very heedful of this argument, but he has no choice. She has asked him for help and he must therefore give it to her, not in a way that pleases her but in accordance with what is for him truth.

It is easy to dismiss Abelard's attitude as cold and lacking in understanding, and it is not difficult to stress at his expense the virtues of the unhappy woman. On the basis of the correspondence, a fierce and yet very reasoned attack could be mounted against monkish piety and grim asceticism. Easy victories of this kind are not however of much value in trying to understand people from past ages. To understand, we must be prepared to accept the fact that people of long ago were able to live their lives on a basis quite different from our own. Through his conversion, Abelard had regained his intellectual integrity on a completely different plane. He had been uncompromising in his own self-absorption and self-admiration, until the meeting with Heloïse destroyed the harmony and flung him into the conflict that was solved for him when, after entering the monastery, he became a monk in earnest. It would be inaccurate to assume that the cause of this transformation is to be found solely in the crime done to him. It is clear that the altered circumstances which flowed from this played an essential part, but Heloïse had already disrupted the undisturbed harmony of his self-absorption. It is probably correct to assume that only through her was Abelard able to draw from the misfortune the conclusions he did in fact draw. She had opened his eyes to concepts greater than Abelard. But, by this, he was led on still further; it was her love that first taught him what love in fact meant. When he tries to come to her help in the correspondence she herself becomes his teacher, as it were. He now sees the knowledge she has imparted to him in a different light. Now he can love her also, but it is a love in Christ; that is to say a love that binds them on their common path towards God, Who has shown them His mercy.

The rest of the correspondence, which we shall not follow here, led to Abelard's making all his learning and attention available to Heloïse and her nuns. It was now a consolation for her to be in touch with him again, but whether she ever succeeded in overcoming her pain and in finding peace in her convent we do not know. The correspondence only tells us that after about thirteen years in the convent she was still the same as when, against her will, she married her beloved. Their positions were – in spite of all the differences – to some extent reversed. Abelard had been freed of the conflict that had tortured him in the marriage, and she, the uncompromising one, was forced into an insoluble schism by very reason of her unswerving fidelity to the synthesis of the heart's urge and the mind's clarity that had always motivated her. The correspondence is far later in date than the dramatic events that led to the separation, and it tells us something of the later attitudes adopted by the two persons concerned. We have no knowledge as to when Abelard reached the conception of his destiny reflected in the letters, but from the autobiography there is reason to believe it took place as early as during the initial period at St Denis.

CHAPTER 4

Disputes and Disappointments

The Benedictine Abbey of St Denis was a dignified old institution closely connected with the French Court. At the time Abelard entered, it was 'unreformed'; that is to say, it was unaffected by the great reform movement that sought to restore monastic discipline in conformity with the entire rigour of the Rule of St Benedict. A few years after Abelard had left the Abbey, Abbott Suger reformed it under the guidance of Bernard of Clairvaux. But in 1119 – probably the year Abelard became a monk – it was still fashionable, rather than scrupulous about the Rule, and more notable for courtly behaviour than for the monastic virtues.[1] The Abbey was probably well pleased that Abelard chose it as his residence. In spite of the scandal and humiliation he was, after all, one of the leading scholars of his time; a man whom even St Denis might feel flattered to include among its monks. This enthusiasm however was by no means mutual. When Abelard discovered that the monks and even the abbot led a life outrageous in relation to their monastic status he was not the man to conceal what he observed. He himself, to be sure, was still in disgrace, but it had never been his intention to enter a monastery to continue a blameworthy life. It is characteristic of him that now he had become a monk he was determined to accept this completely. His duty of course had been made considerably easier for him by the crime whose victim he had been, but even this is not the complete explanation of his zeal. Chastity was no problem for him, but this need not have prevented his enjoying the advantages of the comfort offered by the slack discipline of the order. As a monk, he remained as unyielding and ruthless as he had ever been in his scholarly research. Released from the conflict that had made him falter in the struggle between two passions, he could now once more allow his life to be ruled by the lack of compromise inherent in his nature.

Earlier, he had often had occasion to observe how little other people relish having their attention drawn to their intellectual errors. He now had the same experience in the moral field, for his continual protests against the life of the monastery rapidly made him the object of intense hatred. For the monks therefore it was opportune when the 'clerics', that is to say Abelard's students, urged him to re-establish his school within the monastery. This task required a certain seclusion, and consequently the monks were able to be free of him. The abbot, in giving his permission, probably had in mind the glory that Abelard would shed upon the monastery by continuing his teaching. A house belonging to the Abbey and at the disposal of the abbot was now made available to him, and students gathered here in great numbers. Abelard recounts that the place had neither sufficient living accommodation nor enough food. It was intended that the property concerned should house the students as well as provide their food, but the influx taxed it to breaking point. In their pleas for the school's re-establishment, the students had argued that Abelard should now use his talents for the love of God and 'truly become God's philosopher, rather than the world's'. Whereas he had previously earned much money from his teaching, he should now concern himself with the poor. It is understandable that this line of thought appealed deeply to him. In this way he could once more devote all his time and attention to his real calling, and at the same time see his action as a manifestation of his conversion.

But it was not so much the content of the teaching as its motive that had changed. Abelard recounts that, to match his new position, he devoted most of his attention to theology, but that he did not entirely cease to interest himself in the worldly sciences. He mentions Origen as a model for this dual activity.

in which he used philosophy as a bait to draw his students into the study of 'the true philosophy'. Abelard undoubtedly felt a spiritual affinity with this man, who had sought to create a synthesis between Christianity and Greek philosophy. As already said, there was in general a very lively interest in Origen in the twelfth century. It is probable that Abelard, for other very personal reasons, felt himself attracted to this Greek. He had been in fact a eunuch like himself. In one of his letters to Heloïse he compares himself with Origen, emphasizing also the difference; Origen had castrated himself, whereas Abelard had been overtaken by God's wrath. It is apparent that these are no fortuitous considerations but point to an intense preoccupation with Origen. Consequently there is reason to believe that the knowledge of a common fate increased Abelard's objective interest in him.[2]

When describing his immediate reactions following the crime, Abelard mentions the thought of his enemies' triumph. How delighted they would be over his ill fortune! It is probably true that his rivals now thought they had rid themselves of him once and for all. It is therefore not difficult to imagine the disappointment they must have felt when students once more gathered around him. Unable to withstand his competition or to fight against him, they tried to outmanoeuvre him by technicalities. First, they pointed out that it was incompatible with the duty of a monk to study worldly books; that is to say to occupy oneself with philosophy. Secondly, they maintained that Abelard posed as a teacher of theology without having received authority for this from a master. They therefore had an argument in both of the two fields in which Abelard was occupied. He recounts that they put forward these matters to the clerical authorities with the intention of having him excluded from all teaching. As, apparently, they did not succeed in silencing him his position must have been strong, for both arguments carried considerable weight at the time. For example, the former found enthusiastic support among those within the reform movement. Indeed, it will be seen later that some of Bernard of Clairvaux' indignation towards Abelard was because he, a monk, studied the Greek philosophers. The other point has already been discussed. It was of course true that Abelard had never received an authorization to teach. On the contrary, his only teacher in theology, Anselm of Laon, had forbidden him to conduct theological lectures. However, no regulations appear to have been established at that time.

Another opportunity to get at him soon appeared however. It is very probable that at this time some of Abelard's writings on logic already existed, but as yet no theological work. Not later than 1120 however he wrote a treatise on the Trinity for the use of his students. The manner in which he solved the problem was completely novel. There is no reason to doubt that the book created an enormous stir and became the subject of great admiration, but also of much misgiving. Abelard's fundamental philosophical and theological ideas will be examined in more detail in the next chapter, but it is necessary briefly to refer to a few points here. The new matter in the book can scarcely be expressed more clearly than in Abelard's own words in his reference to it in the autobiography. '.... I ... set out to develop the actual foundation of our belief by means of analogies taken from human reason ...'. As in the treatise itself, he explains in the autobiography that he did so at the request of his pupils 'because they asked for a human and philosophical basis, and preferred something they could understand to mere words. Talk alone was of no use, they said, if it was not accompanied by understanding. Nothing could be believed unless it was first understood, and it was ridiculous for some to preach to others on matters neither they nor their listeners could understand. Besides, the Lord Himself criticized the blind leading the blind.'[3] If one is unacquainted with the history of theology before Abelard, it may be difficult at first glance to see anything sensational in these words. None the less, they express a revolution.

The previous method was that known to Abelard through Anselm of Laon. Authority was explained by means of other authorities. What was new therefore was that the explanation consisted not of different 'words', but of analogies. According to the old method, dogma was 'interpreted' with the help of quotations from the Church Fathers. Abelard also used the Fathers to establish the content of the dogma, but in his view this is merely the beginning. To have meaning for us, dogma must be commensurate with something we know. This is why Abelard used analogies taken from human reason; that is to say, similes from the material world which reason comprehends. There is no question of his believing it possible by means of these analogies, to make dogma evident to reason. Authority is absolutely necessary, but reason must be able to understand what it is that must be accepted on authority. Perhaps his line of thought may be illustrated in the following manner. The 'substance' of the dogma is the Church's doctrine of the Trinity, which is and must be revealed, but its 'form' must be comprehensible to reason. Abelard realizes of course that his analogies will never be anything more than similes, and that they cannot be exact because nothing in this world is precisely equivalent to God, but he believes that this is the only method possible. To the traditionalists this was most disturbing, and there is no doubt whatever it was the method itself that set off his enemies against him.

Among Abelard's contemporaries at Laon were two men who later became masters at Rheims, Alberic and Lotulf. They considered themselves to be Anselm of Laon's heirs, and now saw the Laon tradition threatened. In his autobiography Abelard refers in some detail to their action which led to the convening of a synod at Soissons in 1121, presided over by the papal legate and the Archbishop of Rheims. On the other hand, he is completely silent about another attack. His work – in accordance with his nature – was very polemic. In particular he took great pains to dissociate himself from the teacher of his youth, the notorious Roscelin. It is therefore not surprising that Roscelin, who had already suffered the censure of the Church, considered it necessary to protest. We have no record of his works, but there exists a letter from Abelard to the Bishop of Paris asking the bishop to summon Roscelin so that the matter might be clarified in a disputation.[4] It is doubtful however whether Abelard got anything out of this. In any event, he later tried by different means to attack Roscelin by writing to his colleagues, the canons at St Martin of Tours, to warn them against the old heretic. This letter also is not preserved, but the letter Roscelin sent Abelard on this occasion exists. This letter is hard to equal in coarseness and spite. Roscelin does not refrain from mocking Abelard's disablement and showers insults upon him.[5] However, we do not know what good grounds he might have had for doing this. The whole episode was not of significant importance. Roscelin had a bad name and no influence. It was quite a different matter with the two masters at Rheims.

Unfortunately we are very badly informed about what happened at the Synod of Soissons. No documents or other writings from the synod itself exist. We only know of it through contemporary references, Abelard providing most information. There is no reason here to quote his temperamental account. It is sufficient for us to establish certain fairly definite points. To start with the result, Abelard was sentenced to throw his book on the fire himself, and to permanent detention in the monastery of St Medard, whose abbot was present. The verdict was pronounced without Abelard's having an opportunity to defend himself.[6] They dared not allow him to speak for fear that his eloquence might convince the bishops of the justice of his case. Among these was the respected Geoffrey of Chartres, perhaps the only theologically informed bishop at the assembly. He had in vain appealed to the synod to refrain from convicting Abelard. The papal legate, who can scarcely have had much idea of what it was all about, first seemed inclined to drop the matter but finally decided upon conviction. However, the synod was barely over before he released Abelard from St Medard and allowed him to return to St Denis, which suggests that his conscience cannot have been too clear.

There is consequently no doubt that the synod's conduct was contrary to ecclesiastical law (as Abelard had not been heard) and that the conviction was unjust. For a self-respecting man such as Abelard, it was dreadful to have to humiliate himself, and he writes with great sincerity of his being filled with bitterness against God. In his despair, he thought this to be the worst that had so far befallen him. 'I compared what I had previously suffered in my body with what I had now to tolerate, and considered myself the most unhappy of all men. The treachery then practised I considered insignificant compared with the injustice now done to me, and I lamented much more the injury to my reputation than that suffered by my body. The latter I had inflicted upon myself through my own guilt, whereas the purest intentions and love of our Faith had moved me to write, thereby making me the victim of so manifest an assault.'[7] It appears however that Abelard overestimated the damaging effect upon him of the sentence. On the one hand, his awareness of the injustice of the sentence was deeply felt; on the other hand, it became apparent that it in no way had any effect upon his subsequent teaching activities.

But Abelard's trials were not over with his release from St Medard. A welcome anything but friendly was awaiting him among the brothers at St Denis, who had not forgotten his criticisms of their way of life. With that special talent for arousing opposition which distinguished him, he soon succeeded in giving them further cause for anger. Supported by a passage from the Venerable Bede (673/74–735), one of the most distinguished 'authorities' of the Middle Ages, he expressed doubt as to the accuracy of some information in St Denis' monastic records concerning the founder of the monastery. Patience was now exhausted. Led by the abbot, the monks prepared a complaint to the king, the patron of the monastery, to persuade him to punish Abelard. In this precarious situation, surrounded as he was by enemies, the unhappy man saw no other course but flight. He set out for Champagne, whose count he knew. From there, with the help of friends, he sought to reach an understanding with the monastery. His plan was to get permission to live as a monk in a place of his own choice. To appease the abbot he supported his case by proving in his letter that there was no reason to put one's trust in Bede, as other equally important authorities were in favour of the tradition of the monastery.[8] It is impossible to know whether this letter in fact results from Abelard's having reached a different conviction from that which had stirred up the monks against him, or whether he acted purely from opportunism. It is also possible that he had all along known of the 'authorities' mentioned in the letter, but simply neglected to refer to them earlier so that he might irritate his fellow monks the more!

It proved to be difficult however to obtain the desired permission. In spite of all the animosity towards Abelard, St Denis had no wish to see him join another monastery. The abbot, Adam, died soon afterwards and was succeeded by the famous Suger. He also was reluctant, but through influence at Court he was persuaded in spite of misgivings to grant the permission, with the proviso that Abelard joined no other monastery. He therefore obtained leave to live at a solitary place of his choice, but he was not allowed to join any society of monks.

Abelard chose a remote spot near the town of Troyes, whose bishop gave him permission to erect a small chapel on a piece of ground presented to him. This oratory, constructed from reeds and straw, Abelard named the Paraclete – the Comforter; the name given to the Holy Spirit in the Gospel of St John – because he found comfort and rest there. But by no means was his life to be marked by solitude. The students soon gathered, and before long Abelard's school was flourishing as never before. Nothing can speak more strongly for Abelard's amazing position in the world of learning than the fact that his students followed him into the wilderness. At the same time, it gives a general indication of the simple conditions still prevalent in academic life. Later on it was the schools which attracted the masters, but at the time of Abelard the master was identical with the school. The life unfolding around the Paraclete in the years 1123–1126 would have appeared very odd to us. The students had to build themselves huts to live in. They cultivated the fields and built a new oratory of stone and wood. The miserable hermit's cell was therefore transformed into a large-scale complex of buildings, swarming with youth eager to learn. The realization that neither misfortune nor persecution could impair his reputation nor deprive him of the love of the students gave Abelard new strength. In those years he wrote one book after another, and thus once again gave the world food for thought. But this served also to awaken his enemies from the erroneous belief that he was defeated, and they began once more to consider how they could render him harmless. He gives a very vivid description of living from that time on in constant fear of a new anathema, but unfortunately his account is very vague and we know nothing concrete that might disclose whether this fear was well founded or not. It can scarcely have been completely groundless, since Abelard relates that at one time he even considered going to a heathen country to be permitted to live in peace as a Christian. In his despair, he now received an offer which he believed would put an end to the unrest.

From the monastery of St Gildas de Ruys in far-away Brittany he received an invitation to become its abbot. He obtained permission from St Denis, and then decided to hide himself away in this remote part of the country. As a consequence, he was left in peace by his former enemies, as the school at the Paraclete was of course dissolved and could no longer threaten them. One of Abelard's pupils named Hilarius wrote a lament on the departure of the master. In it he attempts to interpret the sorrow and indignation of the students: 'If you deny us your help, this place will no longer be called a house of prayer (*oratorium*) but a house of lament (*ploratorium*).'⁹ Abelard had no illusions about the life he was entering. 'Thus the same happened to me as to the man who, terrified of the sword threatening him, throws himself into the abyss, and so, to delay one manner of death for a moment, is overtaken by another. In the same way I, with my full knowledge, set out from one danger into another, and there beside the roaring ocean waves where the most distant frontier of the country prevented me from fleeing further I often repeated in my prayers: "From the remotest frontiers of the world I cried to you, while my heart was troubled".' He remained in Brittany as abbot from about 1126 until the early 1130s. It was a dangerous and thankless life, which he was ever about to lose because of the hatred of the uncivilized, covetous and immoral monks. This was his situation in about 1132 when he wrote his autobiography. With his life daily in danger, surrounded as he was by poisoners and blasphemers wearing the monk's cowl, he longed for death as a release.

Although throughout this period Abelard was out of touch with the academic world he was not completely without contact with his old surroundings. He had left the Paraclete, to which while in Brittany he often longed to return, and he was concerned that he had left it without having been able to make provision for the continuation of the divine office. Soon however an opportunity arose for him to make good this deficiency. The abbot of St Denis, Suger, while going through the archives of the abbey, discovered a claim upon the property of the convent of Argenteuil, which he immediately asserted. In 1128 the nuns were driven out. Among these women, now homeless, was their prioress, Heloïse. As soon as Abelard learned of this he handed over to her and some of the nuns his property, the Paraclete, with all its adjoining land. The deed of gift was confirmed in 1131 by Pope Innocent II to the nuns and their successors for ever. Thereafter, the establishment of the new community brought him often to the Paraclete to assist the nuns and to preach to them. In the very middle of his fruitless battle to maintain even an appearance of monastic discipline at St Gildas he had now been given a task which filled him with joy and made great demands upon his energy. It appears that for a short time he dreamt of ending his life at the Paraclete near his wife, as spiritual adviser and preacher to the little community of nuns. But soon malignant accusations concerning his relationship to Heloïse forced him once again to take flight. Although unable to understand the reasons for such suspicion, he retired once more to his unruly monastery. It seems that, as a consequence, the connection between him and Heloïse was broken until she re-established it after reading the autobiography.

In the long succession of years before 1140 we have very little to go on. We do not know precisely when Abelard left St Gildas; only that he did so with the bishop's consent and with the right to retain his rank of abbot. This was probably during 1132 or 1133. Nor do we know what he undertook during the following years until he reappeared in Paris in 1136. But we do know a little about the subject of his thoughts – Heloïse and the Paraclete. After the first passionate letters from Heloïse, and Abelard's reply to them, the entire correspondence concerns the problems of monastic life. Here also Heloïse shows her independence and her brilliant mind. She gives him one problem after another. Theological, liturgical and ethical problems are unrolled, and in deference to her wishes Abelard puts all his energy into helping her to arrive at an understanding. At her request he writes a new rule for the Paraclete. Similarly, he provides hymns to be used during services and sends her sermons. Not in vain did she implore him to help her live the life he had himself decided upon for her. Perhaps we are going too far if we read into this correspondence a suggestion on his part that she had been wrong in believing he had not loved her. But it at least gives the impression that the mutilated man, helpless in the face of a passion he could no longer comprehend, now gives her every-

thing remaining to him, for each is now the only person tying
the other to this world, although in different ways. This desperate attempt to express a love different from and greater than
charity develops in the following correspondence into a gentle
concentration of all his effort. He explains to her that her difficulties give her an opportunity to gain the crown of victory,
while he, as the one released from sensuality, has no crown to
expect. The master admires and loves his pupil, Heloïse. It is
perhaps she who in the end has taught him what his gifts and
his study could not teach – to love and to live.

But this preoccupation with Heloïse and the problems of
monastic life had scarcely at any time dissociated him completely from science. For him, this knowledge was now completely at the service of the life borne witness to in his letters to
Heloïse. This did not mean that his opinions, philosophical and
theological, had changed to any extent, but that they served a
different purpose. Of course, we do not suggest that he had
completely lost his former vanity. We know nothing of this.
But there is no doubt that he was a different man after his
'conversion'. Perhaps during the years that are obscure to us he
examined and revised his earlier writings. In any event, it is
certain that he was to be found once more at Mont Ste Geneviève
in Paris in 1136, where he was heard by among others John of
Salisbury (c. 1120–1180). The long absence appears in no way
to have been a hindrance to him. His reputation reached heights
previously unknown. Young students from all over Europe
gathered to hear him, and his books were spread throughout
many countries. Soon after, however, he disappeared once more
from Paris, but very probably reappeared in the next few years.
We can gain no certain knowledge of his whereabouts before
the attack was commenced that finally defeated him. In this last
battle he found an opponent too strong for him: Bernard of
Clairvaux; This struggle and its consequences will be recounted later. First we must look in more detail at Abelard's
thought, and then examine the motivation of his opponent.

CHAPTER 5

Abelard's Thought

It was as dialectician that Abelard from the very outset won his fame at the Paris schools. His field of activity was very limited, in terms of the educational traditions of the early Middle Ages comprised in the Seven Liberal Arts. Many of his contemporaries possessed a far wider knowledge, but what he may have lacked in range he made up in intensity and depth. The basis of his logic was the same as that of earlier centuries: a couple of Aristotle's treatises on logic – *The Categories* and *On Interpretation* – Porphyry's *Commentary on Aristotle's Theory of Categories*, Boethius' *Commentary on Aristotle and Porphyry*, and Boethius' own treatises on logic. Following the educational tradition, Abelard's logic originally consisted merely of glosses – explanatory notes – on these 'authorities'. In his final work – the *Dialectica* – he attempted a more systematic and independent presentation, but the basis remained the same.[1] It was Porphyry's commentary that presented the problem of universals to the logicians of the Middle Ages. Abelard, in the dispute with William of Champeaux already referred to, solved the problem on the basis of his knowledge of Aristotle. His conception, which will not be developed in detail, impresses one mostly by reason of its formulation upon such a limited knowledge of Aristotle. Abelard was not content to question the validity of William's naïve realism, but went on to draw the logical conclusion by presenting a theory of perception very similar to the viewpoint that became predominant a little less than a century later, when all Aristotle's works had been translated. Against this background, Bernhard Geyer is of the opinion that his penetration into Aristotelean logic and his independent treatment of it was without equal in the twelfth century.[2] With no knowledge of the other areas of Aristotle's philosophy, he succeeded in maintaining the formal character of logic; that is, he kept it free from confusion with metaphysical speculation. A philosophical system in the form of a world view is not to be found in Abelard; neither do we find physical observations based upon experiment. His interest is pure logic, in the sense that he keeps to the investigation of the significance of our concepts and propositions.

It is of course common knowledge that logic was particularly prone to tempt acute minds into an exciting word-play, which could end in idle hair-splitting. This was very clearly recognized even in Abelard's time; for example, one might enter into discussion as to whether the pig being taken to market is pulled by the rope by which it is tied or by the man holding the rope.[3] But Abelard had better things to do than to occupy himself with this kind of 'problem'. The fact that logic is not concerned with matters beyond consciousness but merely with words and sentences certainly did not suggest to him that there is no connection between logic and what really exists, for words and sentences are not empty sounds but expressions of our perception of the reality surrounding us. To occupy oneself with the meaning of words and sentences and their relationship is therefore not an amusement for the quick witted but a rational arrangement of elements, whose association with extramental reality is implicit. While dialectical investigation itself is a purely rational activity – that is to say, is not dependent upon the sensible – its value rests upon the fact that the components with which it works correspond to extra-mental reality. As a true Aristotelean, Abelard stresses that all human understanding is based upon experience. Perception is the first link in understanding; by the activity of the intellect, the formation of the concept occurs by abstraction; the sensory image is torn away from its special circumstances, since the intellect (*ratio*) is able to abstract one part of a number of things, namely that part in which things resemble one another in spite of their individual nature. The universal is therefore not a thing – res – but neither is it 'a nothing'. Through abstraction therefore are formed those concepts with which logic works. From this it follows that it is beyond the interest of dialectic to occupy itself with words and sentences of a fictitious character; that is to say, with words that do not correspond to something actually existing, that do not express an understanding based, in the last instance, upon sensory perception. Idle hair-splitting, in other words, is not to the point. On the other hand, understanding that springs from true dialectic must be itself true in the sense that it corresponds to an extra-mental reality. Assuming the necessary association between the understanding of the concept and the exterior reality, a conviction of the equally necessary 'real character' of the logical conclusion becomes comprehensible. Or perhaps one should rather say: assuming the existence of this conviction, the all-dominating interest in dialectic becomes comprehensible.[4]

Nevertheless, the sense of the words when put together into sentences rests not only upon conformity with an external reality but also upon their relationship. It is in this connection we can see that there is a special element in Abelard's philosophy. Bernhard Geyer expresses the matter thus: 'His philosophy is not a natural philosophy like that of the Chartres school, nor is it an a priori deduction and construction as with Anselm of Canterbury, but a critical analysis of the content of consciousness on the basis of linguistic expression.'

It is as a linguistic logician that Abelard occupies an outstanding position in history. We shall later have an opportunity to follow some of his operations, and we shall therefore do no more here than indicate by an example the importance of linguistic logic. The 'problem' referred to earlier as to whether it is the man or the rope that pulls the pig to market would be rejected immediately by Abelard, not only in the way that a person 'innocent' of logic would reject it as a 'silly' question, but by establishing without difficulty that no problem exists, because 'to pull to market' is not the same in the two sentences that could be formed with 'man' and 'rope' as the subject respectively. Of course! one might very well say; but this was not so obvious in Abelard's time. The example is given here only to add emphasis to what we have tried to point out earlier – that the dialectic to which Abelard gave so much weight was not mere empty verbosity, but was to him a tool, the most distinguished he knew, in his work towards an understanding of human existence.

For Abelard, the function of dialectic is to distinguish between the true and the false. Knowledge of the empirical world stakes out the boundaries of the area within which it is reasonable to attempt to determine whether an opinion is true or false. Grammar safeguards against a formalism which even on the premises of 'physics' can lead to decisions made on a false basis. As an independent science dialectic is purely formal, insofar as its subject is words and their correct use. As an 'applied' science it is a method used on the material of another science. In this sense it is formal insofar as it contributes no new content of any kind but is merely a means of 'understanding' the substance of this other science. Consequently, dialectic is to such a small extent a special enterprise in abstract theory that applied dialectic often became for Abelard a synonym for human reason: *ratio*. Of course he also uses this expression psychologically, but in the present connection it is thought of less as a characteristic of man than as a function, an opportunity to understand.

The basic conception that we have tried to suggest here became of current interest to Abelard when during his stay at Laon he was provoked into giving theological lectures. The manner in which, according to his autobiography, he replied to his opponents shows very clearly that he considered dialectic not merely as a special science but as a method that could be used directly on otherwise unknown material.[5] But in his theological work generally Abelard devotes much space and force to developing his view of the importance of dialectic in theological study. His reflections have given rise to the most varied assessments. He has been enthusiastically acclaimed as the free intellect surrounded by authoritarian, clerical obscurantists, and he has been classified with disgust with the eighteenth-century rationalists. In other quarters – and increasingly in recent research – reference to him as a rationalist has been rejected, if by that term is meant an advocate of the opinion that human reason is competent to evaluate authority – divine Revelation. It is incidentally characteristic that, in this field as in so many others, Abelard has enraged his devotees. He is one of those figures in history whom it is plainly difficult to ignore. He has continually evoked the strongest feelings among both friend and foe. He did so while he was alive, and it appears that he will continue to do so as long as students take an interest in him.

If we are clear about what dialectic meant to Abelard, it is not difficult to arrive at his attitude towards the relationship between theology and dialectic. Dialectic is, for him, in no way a conveyor of truth but an indispensable aid in the understanding and formulation of what is implicit; that is, the content of Revelation. He is sincerely convinced that true dialectic must necessarily serve Faith, for all *artes* are God's gift and consequently must serve Him in spite of the evil thoughts of men. Faith cannot be in opposition to the things created by God and investigated by philosophy.[6] One might say that this line of thought builds upon the conviction that all truth originates in God. In this Abelard agrees with Anselm of Canterbury, who also substantiates his attempt to find reasons for Faith by asserting that truth cannot be opposed to God.

But it would be wrong to conclude from this that Abelard considered it possible to replace, so to say, Faith with reason. There is no question of this. Faith itself is implicit, and it is important to appreciate this to the greatest possible extent. He speaks very clearly of the symbolic character that must characterize all human assertions concerning God.[7] In this connection Abelard's case is far more modest than Anselm's. The great archbishop wished by his understanding to reach beyond Faith; he wished to anticipate, so to say, the eternal beholding of God. Abelard had no thought of anticipating eternity in this manner; unlike the Platonist Anselm, he was more down to earth and could only attempt to interpret, to decipher, Revelation in a language appropriate to the degree of perception that was humanly possible for him. He in no way considered a rational mastery of the divine to be possible for man; in contrast to what might be said of Anselm, there was in his efforts nothing of what the Greeks called *theoria*, speculative insight; contemplation. Rather might it be said that his concern was what theologians of today call 'the hermeneutic problem'; that is to say, his most important purpose was not to reach beyond the spoken word to a higher perception but to *understand* what had been told to the Fathers. It is therefore characteristic of Abelard that he introduces his main theological work, *Theologia*, by saying that he makes no promise to speak truth, but only – following the wishes of his students – to set out his opinion (*opinio*).[8] This phrase later gave rise to Bernard of Clairvaux's indignation, as he considered that Abelard thereby turned Faith into an opinion; that is to say, a not very deeply-rooted conception. But this was not the intention. Abelard wished in no way to question Revelation, but only to distinguish between Faith and the task of theology – the attempt to understand.

The necessity to explain and to defend the use of dialectic in theological work was of course related to the widespread suspicion of dialecticians. Abelard also was very much alive to the false use of dialectic, and he gives strong warning against this. In this connection he enjoyed quoting the Pauline words, that knowledge gives self-conceit, but he asserts that one is misdirected if one concludes from this that there is something amiss with dialectic.[9] He knows of only one effective weapon against the sophisms of pseudo-dialecticians – to fight them on their own ground, that is to say with better and more correct dialectic.[10] It is worth noting that for Abelard dialectic was an inborn gift, and he was no great believer in the possibility of acquiring by diligence and effort what has not been given to one.[11] It is therefore difficult for him to see in the opposition to dialectic anything other than intellectual impotence – the envy of the less endowed towards the gifted.[12] Dialectic must be used as a weapon against lack of Faith. This is a point of view constantly emphasized by Abelard. Dialectic will break down the objections to Revelation, which are of course always false because truth cannot be opposed to God. But dialectic also has a function of a different nature: to teach us to use the authorities correctly.

Abelard embarks upon this most notably in the famous introduction to the treatise *Sic et Non* (Yes and No), in which he sets out his programme for dialectical adjustment between seemingly contradictory authorities. The treatise itself consists entirely of quotations from the Fathers, the liturgy, canon law and the Bible, set out in such a manner that every statement concerning a subject is immediately followed by another having the opposite content. Abelard adds nothing; the solution is left to the reader, who is however shown the proper direction by means of the principles Abelard describes in the introduction. It has sometimes been thought that his intention in this work was to create unrest or to sow doubt. The latter is out of the question, as it would of course conflict with his basic viewpoint, which itself presupposes that conflicting authorities are an impossibility. It is on the other hand justifiable to say that unrest was created in the sense that he wished to give food for thought. He wanted to point out that the authorities as they stand cannot be accepted in intellectual lethargy, but that an effort, intellectual responsibility, is required. Abelard's rules, which include the need for textual criticism (an 'authority' can be adulterated or wrongly quoted) and an investigation of the historical position of the individual authorities (the Fathers, for example, may have had different opinions at different times), will not be gone into here. We shall refer to only one point that is especially characteristic of him: the reference to the fact that conflicting statements are often based upon the different use of words. Sometimes therefore the resolution of the apparent contrast stems from an examination of the context of the statements concerned, using linguistic logic as the only aid.

It is not difficult to follow how Abelard, at first with no hesitation, made use of dialectic in his theology, but gradually found it more and more necessary to defend his method against objections. In the theological treatise burnt at the stake at Soissons – Abelard's first theological work – Roscelin was the main antagonist. Since Roscelin had himself made use of the dialectical method, although in Abelard's opinion with an intellectually worthless and incidentally heretical result, a more detailed justification of the employment of logical argument was unnecessary here. But in later works Abelard is at great pains to substantiate his conception by quotations from the Fathers and by new arguments. One can directly perceive in these writings the truth of the words in his autobiography, where he refers to his constant awareness of the threat of a new anathema over his unpopular head. Although, in spite of this, he continued in the same manner, it was not out of obstinacy but because of an unfailing certainty that his method was correct; a certainty, incidentally, that was in no way shaken by the final judgment on him in 1140. What appeared to his opponents to be impious juggling with the truths of Faith was to Abelard a passion inseparably associated with his personal relationship to Christianity.

In the school of Anselm of Laon, Abelard had missed that dialectical treatment of the verities of the Faith which he himself later attempted to impart, and whose importance he sought to explain in the reflections here referred to. But the traditional attitude was not easy to overcome. In his account of the Synod of Soissons in 1121, Abelard writes of a small episode that may be said to typify the outlook. One of his enemies, Alberic of Rheims, believed one day that he had found a suspicious sentence in Abelard's book, and went to him with some pupils to try to provoke him. When Alberic had disclosed his business, the following characteristic exchange of words took place: '"As far as this is concerned,"³ I replied immediately, "I shall substantiate this rationally, if you so wish." "In this kind of thing," he answered, "we do not care about human reason or our own opinion, but only for the word of an authority." '¹³ Abelard's offer to 'substantiate this rationally' was simply an offer to explain what the disputed sentence *meant* and nothing more. Alberic's reply therefore indicated to him that the other was not interested in the sense but only in 'words'; this as we know was precisely his accusation against their common teacher, Anselm of Laon. For Alberic, the task of theology was to reproduce authority, that is to say to repeat tradition. The independent contribution was mainly in the manner in which the material was arranged. In other words, he stopped at the point where in Abelard's opinion the work began in earnest.

It can be quite enlightening here also to compare Abelard with Anselm of Canterbury. Both of them are concerned with demonstrating why theology cannot remain static with the Fathers, in contrast to traditional theology which wishes merely to reproduce. But how different are their reasons for this! Anselm – in true conformity with the concept of authority –

begins by establishing the absolute unrivalled superiority of the Holy Fathers. How then can he find room for his own work? This he contrives by a reference to the briefness of life: not even the Fathers had enough time to say everything! It is true that they have no equal, but posterity should be allowed to strive after what they did not reach. Apart from this, truth is so wide and deep that no mortal can hope to exhaust it, and although the time of the Fathers is past, the Lord does not cease to be part of His Church.[14] The latter somewhat trivial argument we shall disregard. As concerns the reference to the brevity of life, this is a peculiarly quantitative argument: the holes must be filled up! It is clearly a premise that the work of the Fathers has timeless validity. As to the concept of the width and depth of truth, it should be pointed out that Anselm here demonstrates the exclusive character of theology: it is not a matter of the redeeming truth necessary to everybody, but of truth as an object for contemplation.

Anselm's viewpoint in this matter is very remote from Abelard's. He, Abelard, is not concerned with filling up the holes left by the Fathers nor with arriving at an understanding reaching beyond faith. For him the object of theology is the Catholic faith itself, which to him means: what is necessary for salvation.[15] But if none of Anselm's arguments are of interest to us, why cannot we be content with what the Fathers have written concerning faith? He himself puts this question in one place: of what use was all the discussion of the faith by all these Holy Fathers if there still remains an uncertainty to be discussed? To this he replies: 'It was sufficient for them to solve the problems that came to their notice, to decide the uncertainties of their own times and to leave to their successors an example of how to consider similar problems if they should arise.'[16] In other words: Each era has its problems. The Fathers can provide an answer to nothing but the problems of their own times. For Abelard, the task of theology is therefore determined historically; every age must find its own answers. He therefore succeeded in defining theology in a manner freeing it from Anselm of Canterbury's exclusiveness, as well as from the timeless traditionalism of Anselm of Laon. The starting point is the hermeneutic (interpretative) task, for it was 'ridiculous for anybody to preach to

others about what neither he nor his audience could understand'.[17] But the questions to be answered under the guidance of
the authorities are those of the age itself. Only in this way can
theology fulfil its task. All of Abelard's theological work is
based upon the foundation of faith. He regards himself as an
apologist as against heathens and heretics; at the same time he
sees his theology as concerned with the curing of souls, insofar
as its purpose is the defence of the 'simplicity' (*simplicitas*) of
the faith against the sophists.[18] It is fully apparent to him that
his work is characteristic of the period, and he realizes that it is
important to retain an intellectual composure if analogies and
similes are not to be confused with the substance itself. He has
no wish to use his philosophy to set himself above faith or on a
par with it, but to serve it, because he is convinced that true
philosophy is consistent with Revelation. It is therefore impossible to shake him in his conviction that theology built upon the
artes, above all dialectic, is better than that which is not, that
Paul is a better theologian than Peter and that Augustine is
better than St Martin of Tours.[19]

Abelard succeeded, in a manner superior to and more pointed
than any before him, in formulating a programme for the
employment of dialectic in theology. On the strength of this
programme alone, Abelard stands out as one of the central
figures of the 'renaissance'; since it was his deep penetration into
Aristotelism that made it possible for him to produce his programme. In the conviction that the quality of theology *qua*
theology is dependent upon the degree to which it rests upon
artes – that is to say, classical educational tradition – a Christian
humanism is voiced that was to be of consequence to the content
of his theology. In his attempt to defend the faith against Jews
and heathens he touches upon the heathen philosophers' perception of God.[20] It is basic to him that it has always been man's
own fault if he has not known God and His will. It is therefore
important to establish that the correct perception has always been
available to the heathen world, at least through the medium
of its most outstanding representatives. The next step was of
current interest: by demonstrating that the philosophers con-
formed to the Christian faith, Abelard wishes to refute heretics
and heathens in their attack on Church doctrine. But he has no

interest in the philosophers' theories as such. For example, he has no wish to construct a metaphysic on the basis of Platonic philosophy. The object is entirely apologetic: to refute the suggestion that reason would necessarily lead to a result different from Revelation.

Abelard's knowledge of classical philosophy was however limited. In this field he could derive nothing from Aristotelean logic. He knew Plato's *Timaeus* and some of Cicero's works, but he took most of his material from Christian writers of late Antiquity.[21] It is for him a proven fact that the philosophers knew there was only one God and that they demonstrated by their manner of life that they had the correct perception. It should be noted in this connection that Abelard, like his contemporaries, considered a moral life to be a mandatory prerequisite for correct perception. Consequently, the Fathers' testimony to the pure life of certain philosophers is weighty evidence in favour of the reliability of their intellectual potential. He shows the greatest interest in Plato, in whom he finds the entire Christian doctrine of the Trinity, although not expressed with the same clarity as in the Christian Revelation. In particular he devotes much effort to establishing that the World Soul, *anima mundi*, is the same as the Holy Spirit, which caused much indignation at the time. Abelard's attempt at identification, apart from being rather far-fetched, was bound to raise suspicion because there were many others at the time who occupied themselves with the *anima mundi* concept out of metaphysical interest, with results, such as pantheism, quite alarming in a Christian context.[22] But as we have said, Abelard was quite without such interests. He does not interpret Christianity on the basis of Plato but interprets Plato on the basis of the doctrine of the Holy Spirit. But in fact Abelard gradually changed his opinion in relation to the philosophers. He originally believed that almost all Christian dogma was to be found in them, but later he became more and more inclined to stress the differences.[23]

It is characteristic of Abelard that he concentrated his main theological effort upon what was considered to be most difficult: the doctrine of the Trinity. After he had been forced at Soissons to throw on to the stake his initial work on this, he began once again during his period at the Paraclete. This resulted in a far more extensive work, under the title *Theologia christiana*. Meanwhile, he drafted – perhaps while still at the Paraclete – a plan for a comprehensive and systematic study of the whole doctrine of the faith, of which however he only succeeded in writing the first third. This work – *Theologia* – is in fact a revision of *Theologia christiana*, which is itself very largely based upon the book condemned at Soissons. There is, in the outline and in much of the wording, a clear continuity. We can see in this a very characteristic aspect of Abelard's working method. He repeatedly subjected the book to revision, but in such a manner that he left a great deal standing from edition to edition. The alterations took the form not so much of changes in the wording as of deletions and additions. For example, the first book exists in two versions, *Theologia christiana* in three versions and *Theologia* in as many as five. A similar state of affairs is apparent in his other works.[24] Abelard was the first to use the word 'theology' in the sense it has been used since his time and to this very day. The Fathers never use the word when referring to Christian doctrine, but only about what we call Greco-Roman mythology. The word was therefore heavily encumbered with tradition, and it needed the audacity and inventiveness, not to say the impudence and self-assurance, of someone like Abelard to use it in relation to the 'sacred doctrine', 'the true philosophy', or whatever other expression one was accustomed to.[25]

The word 'Theologia' may have caused some slightly indignant curiosity, but the contents evoked far stronger feelings. It is out of place here to describe in detail Abelard's doctrine of the Trinity, but it is necessary for us to concern ourselves with certain aspects of it if we are to understand the dispute to which it gave rise. The Church doctrine on the Trinity was, as we know, developed in ancient times and acquired its more detailed elaboration through a number of dogmatic disputes. In Latin Christianity, Augustine's great work *On the Trinity* came to be accepted as the conclusive synthesis of clerico-orthodox doctrine, and consequently as a guide for the theology of the Middle Ages. As the dogma had long been established from a canonical aspect, there was no longer a free field of action here for the theologians. Their concern could only be to render as faithfully as possible the dogma that taught of three Persons in one deity. The Persons were equal in every respect, indeed they were One, only separated in their relation to one another as Persons. The whole dogma rests upon a subtle philosophical conceptual apparatus of which a present-day person can probably acquire only a quite superficial understanding, although it must be stressed that this is not to say that the dogma possesses no comprehensible human element. Although Abelard and his contemporaries were familiar with this form of the dogma, this is not to say they had no inkling of the difficulties.

For this reason, by far the greater part of the space Abelard devotes to the doctrine of the Trinity is taken up by explanations. The Church doctrine itself he puts forward briefly, clearly and correctly. But in accordance with his methodical principles he believes that the explanation is more important. 'What indeed is the use of talking in order to teach if what we wish to teach cannot be explained so that it can be understood?'[26] And how is such an explanation to be effected? This can be done only with the aid of examples and similes. To explain is to compare the dogma, or what forms part of it, with known things. As an explanation must not only illuminate the dogma but also refute the enemies of Christ, examples and similes must be taken from a field recognized by these enemies; that is to say, from the sciences.[27] Authority, the dogma, is absolute, the foundation, and precedes the arguments, which must be viewed as the 'buttresses' (fulcimenta). They are added so that the enemies of Christ cannot by their verbosity mock the simplicity of faith.[28] They submit only to reason, and they must therefore be answered by one well versed in the sciences from which they take their arguments. The question now is: to what extent is this project possible, and what is it that one may hope in this way to substantiate by reason?

Abelard in no way tries to conceal the difficulty that arises from God's being infinitely different from everything else and therefore from everything we know of. God is the absolutely unique One for Whom the potentialities of language are truly insufficient. Words, Abelard believes, are formed by man to describe his understanding of created things. Language is, so to speak, determined by our temporality. It is therefore not surprising that God goes far beyond what we can express and understand. We have no vocabulary specifically suited to God, and therefore everything we say about Him has a figurative, metaphorical meaning.[29] In spite of these difficulties, which in truth perhaps end in the impossible, the attempt must be made. But awareness of the conditions underlying this attempt also leads to an assessment of the scope of the attempt, and this demands our interest.

The consequence of the 'incompetence' of language is that interpretation of the dogma, which is carried out with the aid of examples and similes, must lack the precise nature that characterizes our understanding of created things. But to interpret the dogma in this manner Abelard calls 'justifying by reason'. It therefore appears that 'justifying by reason' is the same as using pictures, that is to say the examples and similes referred to. Against this background it becomes comprehensible that Abelard can say: '... we certainly do not promise to teach the truth, which we believe is beyond the attainment of us or any other mortal; but we do at least wish to present something that is similar to truth (*verisimili*), something that accords with human reason without conflicting with the sacred faith, turned against those who boast of fighting the faith with human arguments – they care for nothing but human arguments which they know, and they readily find many followers, since almost all men are unintellectual and only very few are intellectual'.[30] These sentences apply solely to Abelard's attempt to interpret Revelation. He will only promise to produce something similar to the truth, because no simile is identical with the matter itself, and he can give nothing but similies, for ' ... faith is a conviction of that which we cannot see'; that is to say, that which cannot be made the object of perception founded upon sensation. 'It is one thing to understand or believe, but another to perceive or clarify.'[31] Abelard does not confuse his understanding, his interpretation of Revelation, with 'scientific' perception, but it is for him a necessity to understand, that is to say interpret, the language of divine authority in a manner analogous to what we as men know.

Abelard's thoughts on the Trinity are based upon the old tradition, in that he applies the concepts of power, wisdom and goodness to the Father, the Son and the Holy Ghost respectively. The name of the Father expresses in particular the power of the divine majesty: that He can do whatever He wishes. The name of the Son or the Word signifies the wisdom of God, by which He can see through everything and can be deceived by nothing. The Holy Ghost expresses the goodness of God, by which He accomplishes everything in the optimum manner. Therefore, Abelard believes, the Trinity embraces the whole divine perfection.[32] He presents at great length a 'proof from authority' that the three divine names truly express God's power, wisdom and goodness respectively, and he then refers to the philosophers, particularly Plato. But the real problem still remains. How can there be in God several Persons separate from one another, if it has been established that God is an indivisible unity? Tradition maintains that the Persons are separated as concerns their relationship: what is peculiar to the Father is to be 'unborn', that is to say to have His being from Himself and not from another; the Son is characterized by being born of the Father, not created; and the Holy Ghost 'proceeds' from both the Father and the Son. As we have seen, Abelard makes no claim to demonstrate the truth of this doctrine, but he wishes with the aid of a few similes to make the relationship between the Persons intelligible. Nothing but authority can say that *this* is how God *is*, but we can try to find something in this world that is similar to what authority says about God. This is of what interpretation of the dogma consists.

Abelard presents many different images, but we shall only describe here the one he preferred. A seal is made of bronze. When the image of the king has been formed in the material, the seal is ready for use as a seal (*sigillabile*) even if it is not yet in use as a seal (*sigillans*). But when the wax is sealed with it we then find that there are three things in this one substance which are different as concerns their attributes; that is to say the bronze, the seal (*sigillabile*) and the sealing itself (*sigillans*). These three are mutually connected in the sense that the seal has proceeded from the bronze, and the sealing, for its part, from bronze and seal in association. In this way the image is ready for use: in the same way as the seal has its bronze nature from the bronze, so the Son has His being from the Father (*ex substantia* patris) and is said to be born of Him. Now, as we have already said, the name of the Father indicates to us especially the power of God, and that of the Son His wisdom. Consequently, Abelard believes, it can be said that wisdom is 'a certain power', in the same way as the seal is 'some bronze'. The wisdom is the power by which God sees through everything and can err in nothing. That the Son is born of the Father is therefore the same as saying that the wisdom is equivalent to the power to discern, that it has its being from the power of the Father and therefore is a kind of power itself. In order to avert the possible misunderstanding that he was in this way making the Son subsequent to the Father, which would be opposed to Church dogma, Abelard now finally points out that the power in no way goes before the wisdom, as the one is unthinkable without the other.[33]

He then continues by discussing the 'proceeding' of the Holy Ghost. He begins by demonstrating that goodness, as its name suggests, is not power or wisdom in God but rather His love which He reaches out towards another. From this basis Abelard now tries to show wherein lies the difference between the birth of the Son and the proceeding of the Holy Ghost. He Who is born is of the substance of the Father (ex substantia patris), which Abelard has shown by pointing out that wisdom is 'a certain' power. It is otherwise with the One Who 'proceeds', for the passion of love has more to do with goodness of the spirit than with power. Abelard therefore does not believe – in spite of certain Fathers – that one may say that the Holy Ghost is of the Father's substance, even though Father, Son and Holy Ghost are one and the same substance. Indeed, if one asserts this there is no difference between being born and proceeding, and it has then not been understood what separates the Son and the Holy Ghost from one another. The statement in the dogma that the Holy Ghost has proceeded from the Father and the Son means therefore that the Holy Ghost is the unity of love between Them.

But then God in His perfection is in need of nothing. He therefore turns in His goodness towards created beings who need Him. But this goodness towards creation rests upon power and wisdom. If goodwill towards creation is to accomplish anything, the power to do so and the knowledge of how to do it is necessary. Therefore, the Holy Ghost proceeds from both the Father and the Son. Abelard now employs his simile once more: bronze, seal and sealing are different in their attributes, that is to say in their manner of existing in relation to one another, in the same way as are the Father, the Son and the Holy Ghost; but they are of the same essence. Abelard finally stresses, in conformity with tradition, that the Almighty is of course both wise and good, but that this does not mean that the Father *is* the Son or the Holy Ghost. His use of the terms, power, wisdom and goodness, to characterize the relationship of the three Persons is therefore not intended to question the orthodox doctrine of the absolute equality of the Persons.[34]

Although Abelard's simile will scarcely make the primitive Church's dogma of the Trinity more understandable to a modern reader, it was for several reasons necessary to show here how his method was pursued. We are of course not concerned here with the dogma of the Trinity itself, but solely with Abelard's thought. What matters therefore is not whether his reasoning makes any impression today but how he wished to employ it. It is necessary to be absolutely clear about this if we are to understand the dispute to which his theology gave rise and its historico-intellectual background, which will be described later. What is it he wishes to make comprehensible with the aid of the seal image. It is *solely* the relationship between the Persons. Abelard, in accordance with Church doctrine, postulates and continues to repeat that God is one indivisible substance, and that all characteristics that do not concern the relationship between the Persons are common to all three Persons. But the characteristics that concern the relationship between the Persons are those and those alone that express themselves in their manner of existing in relation to one another: that the Father is the unborn, the Son the one born of the Father, and the Holy Ghost the One proceeding from the Father and the Son. Although Abelard uses the terms, power, wisdom and goodness, to characterize the three Persons, he stresses that the son is omnipotent on the same level as the Father and the Holy Ghost, the Father is wise on the same level as the Son and the Holy Ghost, etcetera. But the simile should not be employed to express this similarity and unity; it should only express the difference: that

which makes it necessary to speak of three Persons although
there is only one God. If the simile is used differently it can lead
to fatal consequences, but Abelard certainly does not do this.
On the contrary, he says in one place that any simile applies to
one part alone and never to the whole, because it is a fact
that what is equal to something else (but implicitly not the same)
is unequal to this other thing in some respects.[35] It is therefore
necessary to know exactly how one wishes to employ one's
simile and how one does not wish to employ it.

One leading authority on Abelard, J. G. Sikes, rightly points
out that Augustine's *On the Trinity* is the basis of Abelard's
doctrine. He adds that Abelard, in contrast to many of his contemporaries, was unable to reproduce what Sikes calls 'the
metaphysical greatness of that book.'[36] This is of course one way
of expressing it. But one might also say that Abelard's discussion of the doctrine of the Trinity reveals none of that wider
interest that might have tempted him to reproduce Augustine's
metaphysical thought. His tool is dialectic alone and his material
is Church dogma alone. His intention is not to reach beyond the
dogma to a higher insight, but only to understand the dogma
and at the same time to fight against false teachers. The means
to this is solely interpretation; not explanation in the sense of a
rational mastery of Church doctrine. Abelard, as an empirical
Aristotelean, considered such an approach to be not only impossible but also contrary to the faith. Whatever reason is compelled to recognize has nothing to do with faith, and is therefore
of no merit to God.[37] Confronted with the enemies of Christ, he
therefore has no hope of producing an irrefutable proof of his
case, but merely of destroying their self-assurance when they
assert that reason is contrary to faith.

Anselm of Canterbury, as we know, had tried to prove the
existence of God. Abelard also asks whether it is possible by the
use of reason to apprehend that there is only one God. He does
not go to much trouble over this question, and it is clear that he
considered it not to be any problem. He reminds us that it
is characteristic of reason to investigate those things that the
senses cannot comprehend, and he points out that reason is the
special proof of the God-image of man and should therefore have
the potential of comprehending God, Whom it resembles. God

can be recognized, Abelard believes, in His work, as can the artist in his. He also brings into the discussion the writers of Antiquity, Cicero and Plato in particular.[38] But he is much more concerned with the question of God's omnipotence. Can God do more and better things than He does? Abelard is inclined to answer: No. God does everything in the optimum manner and for the most reasonable cause. Although he is fully aware that most authorities say otherwise, Abelard still believes that God can only do what is proper to Him, and that whatever He leaves undone is not proper to Him. If one objects that God's sublimity is thereby reduced, for even we who are so much weaker can do many things that we do not do, he replies: this has nothing to do with the power of God. This 'ability' of ours is not merit but rather weakness, for we should be better if we could only do what we should do.[39]

Another important problem, which had also occupied Anselm of Canterbury, was the question of God's prescience and providence. God is unchanging and therefore has possessed all knowledge from eternity. Does this now mean that everything occurs inevitably? Abelard believes he has found in Aristotle the arguments that can dissolve the sophisms of the pseudo-philosophers, whereby they tend to confuse simple people's faith in God's providence by saying that not only good things but also evil things occur inevitably. Abelard starts from the principles of contradiction: it applies to every affirmative and negative that one of them is necessarily true. For example, the sentences: The battle at sea will take place tomorrow, and: The battle at sea will not take place tomorrow. One of the sentences is necessarily true and the other false, for they cannot both be true; and it is not possible for both of them to be false. But a distinction must now be made between two kinds of necessity: it is necessary for the battle either to take place or not to take place tomorrow, but it does not follow from this that it will necessarily take place or that it will necessarily not take place. On this basis, Abelard believes it to be possible to demonstrate that God's prescience imposes no determination upon events, any more than does our prescience or knowledge. If I watch a person writing, it is necessary that he does so, but my observation does not compel him to do so.[40]

Abelard's view of the omnipotence and prescience of God is here presented very briefly to show a certain type of reasoning that stems from a conviction of the 'realistic character' of logic. Against the background of certain established factors – God's immutability, omnipotence, etc. – it is only necessary to deduce in the correct manner to be certain of arriving at a correct result. We are concerned here with a far more direct use of dialectic than in the doctrine of the Trinity, and it is associated with the fact that the question here is God's relationship, not to Himself but to the world. The concepts of God used here are related at the outset to something we know; power, know-ledge, etcetera. It is therefore only necessary to postulate these concepts to their absolute maximum and then to draw the logical conclusions.

Abelard never succeeded in finishing his main work. *Theologia* exists in three books, of which the first two discuss the doctrine of the Trinity and the last the questions just referred to, with a few others of the same nature.[41] From other writings, in particular the *Commentary on the Epistle to the Romans* and the *Ethics*, we can only to a very limited extent form an impression of what might have been contained in the two missing main sections: on 'The Divine Benefaction' (Christ and His Works) and 'The Divine Institutions' (particularly the Sacraments). In the *Commentary on the Epistle to the Romans* there is a paragraph on the Atonement, which may be taken as a study for the corresponding section in *Theologia*. Abelard poses the question: What is meant by our atonement through the death of Christ? The doctrine of the atonement had not been canonically established in the same manner as the doctrine of the Trinity for example, but it may be said that a definite line in clerical tradition was prevalent. Since the time of the primitive Church, great weight had been given to the part played by the Devil. It was generally asserted – following Gregory the Great, whose influence in this field as in so many others was very considerable in the Middle Ages – that the Devil, through sin, had obtained some kind of right over man. When he believed that he could also gain the upper hand over Jesus he was defeated. When he profaned the pure soul of Jesus, which he could not secure, he lost his right over man. This strange theory had been opposed before Abelard's time by Anselm of Canterbury, who elaborated a new doctrine of atonement, the so-called doctrine of satisfaction or doctrine of objective atonement. But Abelard, in his criticism of the traditional doctrine as well as in the suggestion he puts in its place, appears to have been completely unaffected by Anselm.

To Abelard, the idea of the Devil's right appears quite absurd. The tempter who entices away another person's servant does not thereby secure any right over him. The only kind of right the Devil may have had could only have been as God's jailer or executioner! But, Abelard says, it would be easy for God to forgive man his sins, and the executioner would then have no right. But then the question remains: If it were easy for God to have freed man from the Devil, why had the Son of God to take upon Himself all the suffering and humiliation He had to endure? How can Paul believe that we are justified through His death, for it is easier to believe that God would be the more angry with man, who killed Him? Can it be that His innocent death could have pleased God the Father so much that He was thereby reconciled with us who, through our sin, were guilty of His death? While Anselm sees Jesus' suffering as a reparation for the revolt against God (which assails His honour), so settling the score, it is impossible for Abelard to propound any settlement: 'But however cruel and unjust it may appear that one person should demand as payment the blood of an innocent person, or that it should in any way please him that an innocent person is killed, how much less would God find pleasure in the death of His Son in order that He might thereby be reconciled with the world?'[42]

As an alternative to this conception, Abelard advances the idea that the atonement is the revelation of God's love expressed in the fact that Christ became man, taught us by His word and example and persevered unto death. By proclaiming this act, or rather by faith in Christ, love of God Who first loved us is awakened in our hearts so that we are freed from the power of sin and the Devil: 'Our redemption is therefore this greatest love in us through Christ's suffering, the love which not only delivers us from the bondage of sin but gains for us the true freedom of God's children, so that we, rather through love of Him than fear, fulfil all; He Who has shown us such great mercy that none greater exists, as He himself witnessed: "Greater love, He says, hath no man than this, that a man lay down his life for his friends." [43] For Abelard, therefore, Redemption is the proclamation of God's love in Jesus' life and death as a transforming power through faith. Unfortunately he never succeeded in writing a detailed account of this doctrine of atonement, but on the basis of what we have it is possible to draw conclusions that are characteristic of Abelard's thought.

Abelard begins by asking: by what necessity did the Son of God become man in order to redeem us? We have seen that, unlike Anselm, he has no wish to answer this question by treating Christ's work as a logical necessity; in his opinion, God could have forgiven sin without difficulty. Nevertheless, Abelard does not seriously consider other possibilities, and this probably stems from his belief that God always does precisely what is appropriate to Him. Abelard therefore acknowledges the factual necessity: this was how it happened and we must accept it. But he must then try to understand the redemption in a manner not involving the logical necessity. One might also say that the possibility he himself refers to – that God could have forgiven without difficulty – gives him a clue that the content of the actual redemption through the blood of Christ must include the same elements as a hypothetical redemption through the forgiving Word alone. Abelard is therefore not really interested in the concept of substitute suffering, which became a main point in Anselm's doctrine of atonement, as this concept was of course associated with that very method, that is to say with Christ's death upon the cross. But if the redemption is to correspond to the imagined possibility – redemption through the Word – the emphasis cannot be on some form of payment or any other external thing, but must lie in something spiritual. In this way Abelard arrives at the conclusion that the decisive factor must be the revelation of God's love. This is not the place to discuss the theological consequences of this doctrine in a wider context; it appears in Abelard's writings only as a first draft, which must be read primarily in contrast to tradition's preoccupation with the rights of the Devil. This in itself is an impressive independent effort of thought.

There is no reason to assume that Abelard would have changed

his mind if he had had time to write on the atonement in
Theologia, because the fundamental viewpoint – that the
redemption must be of a spiritual nature – is closely akin to his
basic thought on ethics as developed in the strange little book
bearing the title Ethica or Scito te ipsum; that is, 'Know thyself'. This is perhaps the most original of Abelard's works. Here
he consistently puts forward the conception we have encountered earlier in Heloïse's letters: the goodness or wickedness of
our actions is dependent upon the intention alone. One must
face the fact that this led him into opinions that in no way
coincided with the average view of morality! This may be illustrated by a few examples. Abelard asserts that sin consists solely
in consenting to the contempt of God, and shows itself in that
we do not do for His sake what we believe we should do, or in
that we do not abstain from doing what we think we should
abstain from for His sake.[44] This he compares with the objection
of others that an evil will is also sin. In this connection, Abelard
understands them to mean, by 'will', lust and desire. He refutes
the objection, saying that when the law orders us not to covet,
the meaning is: not to consent to covetousness.[45] Others, he says,
are disturbed by his assertion that the sinful action does not
increase the guilt that is associated with sin. This cannot be
right, they say, for the action is associated with a joy which in
itself is sinful. Abelard however disputes that the joy associated
with intercourse with women or eating a good meal, for example,
could in itself be anything sinful. This joy arises of necessity,
but as it is necessary to eat and marriage is permissible – indeed
plainly commanded in the Old Testament – it is quite unreasonable to believe that the joy which is part of it should be sinful.[46]
On the whole, the soul cannot be sullied by anything that
occurs because of the body, but only by that which occurs to
the soul itself; that is to say by consent to what is contempt of
God, whether or not it occurs before the act or together with it.
On the other hand, we often do things that are not right without thereby sinning, for example when we act under compulsion
or from ignorance. It is not necessarily sinful to covet another's
wife or to sleep with her (one might be compelled, or deceived
into believing that she is one's own wife!), but it is sinful to
consent to the desire or the act.[47]

Sin therefore rests with the intention alone. The same action can at different times be good or evil, according to the intention. It is nevertheless important to appreciate that a good intention is not that which considers itself to be good but only that which is good in itself, that is to say in accordance with the will of God; otherwise unbelievers would be able to do good deeds.[48] But, as Abelard is of the opinion that ignorance excuses, to come to terms with the unbelievers is a dilemma for him. For example, those who persecuted the martyrs and Christ acted according to their conscience, and for this reason one cannot call their actions sinful; they did what their conscience bade them do.[49] An attempt to go further by distinguishing between sin in the actual sense and in a number of metaphorical senses does not help him over the problem. His principle prevents Abelard from calling disbelief sin in the true meaning when it is a consequence of ignorance, and yet he must insist, with Church doctrine, that not to believe in the Gospel leads to perdition.[50] He knows no real answer to this question. But in this connection we must remember his interest in the lives and beliefs of the philosophers. As concerns his ethic, the important factor here is that we are confronted with a real attempt in principle to take up a position on the question: what is it that makes our actions good or evil? The discussion in its entirety is on a level far above the moral considerations generally to be found in Church literature of earlier times. Problems were raised here that future generations were obliged to investigate.

For the moment however we shall concern ourselves more with the contemporary attitude to Abelard's work. It was first of all his theological works that gave cause for discussion. In philosophy – that is, dialectic – he was generally acknowledged to be the foremost of his period. On the other hand his return to the academic world in 1136 led to his involvement in his last great dispute. It was as if all the forces that had earlier opposed him now gathered with renewed strength. This time traditionalism was able to enlist on its side the most influential personality of the Church in France, perhaps in all Christendom: Bernard of Clairvaux. Before we examine the dispute and its consequences, it will therefore be necessary to take a look at this man.

CHAPTER 6

Bernard of Clairvaux

Bernard was born in 1090, the son of a Burgundian nobleman and a pious mother who died young, but who exercised much influence on his childhood. He had five brothers and one sister, all of whom, including Bernard, ended their lives as religious. When he was twenty-one he decided, following the wishes of his dead mother, to enter a monastery, and in 1112, accompanied by four of his brothers and twenty-five friends, he presented himself at the struggling new foundation of Cîteaux. Founded by Robert of Molesme, who had sought in vain to achieve his ideal of 'evangelical perfection' in other houses, Cîteaux was then under its third abbot, the Englishman Stephen Harding. In 1112 Cîteaux was still an impoverished community with an uncertain future. For the house, the arrival of Bernard's party was decisive, and its phenomenal growth dates from that moment. For Bernard the moment was equally decisive.

Most monasteries of the time followed the rule of St Benedict of Nursia who, demanding *stabilitas* – the obligation that the monk should remain in the house he had joined – from his monks, had effected a threefold division of the day – into the *opus Dei* (the daily round of the canonical hours), *opus manuum* (manual labour) and *lectio divina* (spiritual reading and study). The triple vow of the Benedictine monk was to chastity, poverty and absolute obedience. As a way of life it was disciplined, and of moderate and reasonable asceticism. With the passage of time, however, it became overlaid with supplementary customs which varied from house to house, and underwent one major alteration with the disappearance from the daily timetable of manual labour in the fields. At the time of the foundation of Cîteaux many, though by no means all, Benedictine houses belonged to the congregation of Cluny, in which most attention was given to the performance of an elaborate and much enlarged liturgy. At Cîteaux however, as at other foundations of the period, there was a return to the primitive simplicity of the Rule, and indeed to yet earlier exemplars. The Cistercians looked not only to Benedict but also to the Egyptian desert Fathers of the third and fourth centuries, whose way of life was known to them from the descriptions of Gregory the Great, among other sources. Here they found an ideal of life which prescribed not merely a moderate asceticism with the object of preventing satisfaction of the senses from coming to the fore but demanded an active struggle to obliterate any – even the smallest – physical enjoyment. This was achieved by reducing food to a minimum, depriving it of all flavour by forbidding the use of spices in its preparation, by banning comfortable clothes and by prescribing a hard uncomfortable bed. At Cîteaux, physical work once again became the rule, and this in itself was a considerable penance. Prayer, cut to the minimum, at the canonical hours took up about six hours of the day. The remainder of the day was divided between intellectual and physical work. This programme was designed to reproduce what was considered to be the way of life of the early Church.

It is easy enough now to decry all this, but it must be remembered that, although the degree of outward asceticism was often the subject of dispute in the twelfth century, asceticism for the Cistercians was not an end in itself. Its object was to create the necessary conditions for the humility that was to free the spirit for a life in God. By this means, however curious and alien it may seem to us, they sought to attain *freedom*. There is no doubt that Bernard entered wholeheartedly into the struggle that the rule prescribed for him, and there is also no doubt that he found ways to intensify in his own case the already almost inhuman regulations. It is said of him that he was soon in control of his senses to such a degree that he neither saw nor heard in the course of his daily life anything irrelevant to the aim he had set himself – evangelical perfection. The intellectual life of the twelfth century has rightly been spoken of as a 'rediscovery of nature' in the fields of both science and poetry, but for all his intellectual gifts it may reasonably be said that Bernard stood wholly apart from this revival. The Order was not satisfied to forbid all personal sensual pleasures in the form of physical enjoyment, but was opposed to the materially beautiful itself. Ornamentation of Cistercian churches was consequently strictly forbidden. All such things were considered to be inimical to the mortification and purification of the flesh; indeed it might be said that anything not directly serving this end was viewed as useless and dangerous. As a consequence, the new Order could of course attach no importance to study, except as an adjunct to the performance of the demands of the Cistercian life. The Bible was read, as were the Fathers and the lives of the saints, but simply as a necessary part of the personal quest for perfection. Knowledge and pursuit of learning which had no connection with this end attracted the same aversion as beauty.

But these principles could not prevent individuals within the Order from contributing to the culture of the period. It must not be forgotten that many of its members were highly cultured men who, in spite of their desire to leave behind them everything associated with the world, were unable to deny the culture they had acquired before entering the monastery.

When Bernard entered Cîteaux, the monastery was in the middle of a crisis. Many of the monks had recently died in an epidemic, and recruits had been deterred from entering the house by the rigour of its life. But from now onward there began a tremendous flowering which in the following years made necessary the foundation of daughter houses. La Ferté and Pontigny were the first two, and in 1115 Bernard was chosen as abbot of the third, Clairvaux. Together with twelve monks, among whom were two of his brothers, he left Cîteaux, and for some years he was fully occupied with the organization of the monastery that, because of him, was soon to be famous throughout Europe. The new foundation was initially extremely poor, and it was some years before its lands were able to yield even the little the monks needed. In the course of time, Clairvaux became immensely rich, but this had not the slightest effect upon the way of life of the monks. With the increase in wealth, the number of monks and lay brothers also increased, and towards the end of Bernard's life it is said to have reached about 700. In the same period the abbey spread its daughter houses throughout Europe, founding sixty-eight during Bernard's abbacy.

This great increase was not of course accidental; throughout his life, Bernard was very active in 'converting' clerics and laymen. As we said earlier, conversion (*conversio*) was the designation by which the transition from a life in the world to the cloister was characterized. The biographical accounts are full of descriptions of how Bernard on many different occasions returned to Clairvaux with a retinue of the newly converted, who had decided to leave the world after hearing him preach. It was of course inevitable that this kind of event was rumoured far and wide. As a result, many who had never heard or seen Bernard found their way to Clairvaux. Among these were many monks from older orders who felt impelled to choose a stricter rule. But as a consequence the success of the new order became a matter that affected these older Orders; comparisons were of course made between the Cistercians and the other Benedictines. This very soon led to a conflict between the Cistercians and the powerful Cluniac congregation, which had received in 1122 as abbot of Cluny a new and outstanding leader in the person of the famous Peter the Venerable.

By the time the new Order had reached a certain degree of dissemination, its interpretation of Benedict's rule came of necessity to be looked upon as a criticism of the black monks, as the other Benedictines were called to distinguish them from the white Cistercians. Very soon, as might be expected, this criticism became so voluble that Peter the Venerable considered it necessary to speak his mind. In a letter quite clearly aimed at Bernard – the principal behind the success of this new Order – he accused the Cistercians of Pharisaism and defended in detail the Cluniac interpretation of the rule according to the spirit and not according to the letter, 'which kills'. Bernard, who had not so far taken part directly in the polemics, now wrote his *Apologia*, in which he severely condemned those Pharisees among the Cistercians who allowed themselves to depreciate the

Cluniacs. But at the same time he succeeded in presenting a destructive criticism of Cluniac practices. He carefully reviewed Cluniac customs in relation to meals and clothing, and their way of life in general. He sharply rejected their artistic interests as unworthy of monks, who should flee from all luxury. In spite of his anxiety to show respect for the older Order, Bernard cannot hide the fact that he finds many grave faults in their way of life. Although Peter the Venerable very soon initiated extensive reforms within his congregation, striving for greater simplicity in the Cluniac way of life, the differences were and remained great, and a certain bitterness which flared up from time to time into real hostility was long prevalent between the two Orders. At Cluny, an ascetic austerity in food and clothing was not considered necessary for nor appropriate to true monastic life. For example, it is characteristic of the difference between them that Peter, in contrast to Bernard, lavished much care on the physical health of his monks. In the matter of work, within the Cistercian Order the whole emphasis was on physical work, whereas this was an exception with the Cluniacs, who put liturgical and artistic activities above all else. The spirit was so different in the two places that conflict was inevitable.

Bernard's zeal for very strict monastic discipline not only determined his outward activity but eventually led to the destruction of his health. After a very few years he was so prostrated that it became necessary, to save his life, to relieve him of the leadership of the monastery completely for one year. He never wholly recovered, but suffered until his death from digestive complaints. But he succeeded in using this also as an element of mortification, and in later life the illness appears to have been unable to prevent his unceasing work. About 1130, Bernard was able to write, 'the world is full of monks!' By saying this, he was not only calling attention to the fact but voicing a jubilant declaration that a vital endeavour had succeeded in progressing. It was certainly his aim to rob the world of as many souls as possible, and he used all means to this end: encouragement, warnings, threats and reproaches. As we have said, he made no attempt to conceal that, for him, the Cistercian Order, since it was the Order that made the greatest effort towards perfection, took first place. He therefore always permitted transfers from other Orders to his own, although in principle he was opposed to any breach of stability. But such cases, he believed, were new 'conversions' to a life of still greater humility. However, he recruited by far the greater number of his novices directly from 'the world'. But although he gave his own Order pride of place he was fully aware that its demands lay at the limit of human endurance. His level-headedness was such that he not only sought to obtain new supporters for the Order but did all he could to promote reform within the other Orders.

There is only space here to refer to the most important aspects of his activity in very general terms. During the 1120s his reputation was greatly enhanced by the miraculous cures he was reported to have performed. A large number of Benedictine monasteries were reformed during this period, and in many cases Bernard had a finger in the pie. He was equally active with the canonical clergy. In cathedral churches and many other great churches there were a varying number of canonical offices. The holders of these offices could either live as secular canons, independently of one another, each on his own prebend, or as 'regular' canons; that is to say, subject to a rule in a communal life reminiscent of a monastery. As might be expected, Bernard worked eagerly to promote the regular life among canons, and among these there were two Orders in particular which enjoyed his favour because of their relative austerity of life: the Victorines and the Premonstratensians. In those places where he did not succeed in establishing a regular way of life, he sought to exercise his influence upon the clergy by persuading them to give up all luxuries. He also tried to influence bishops and other clerical dignitaries, and a number of bishops were 'converted' through his efforts. In many instances his ideals also caused him to turn on the great secular nobles of the period to warn them or threaten them if for one or another political reason they pursued aims that, in Bernard's opinion, stood in the way of his reformative work. In other words, he entered into Church politics on a large scale. He did not hesitate to call upon the secular power when he thought it could support reform with other and more tangible arguments, after his own had proved ineffective. He very soon came into contact with the ruling prince in whose lands Clairvaux lay, the powerful and pious

Count Theobald of Champagne, and exercised considerable influence over him. But he also had the effrontery to direct even the most powerful: both the Pope and the King of France found themselves receiving instructions from him. It is easy for later generations to see that as early as the 1120s Bernard possessed considerable political influence, and that in the following years he attained an unparalleled position. But his contemporaries also were well aware of this. It was asked: by what right did an ordinary abbot delude himself into believing that it was his duty to guide the Church in all France? How could he allow himself to interfere in the affairs of bishops and princes; indeed even in those of the Pope and Curia?

To Bernard, the answer was quite simple. He spoke in the name of reform. 'Nothing of what concerns God is alien to me,' he wrote to a cardinal. God's business was always his business; this was how he saw it. On the basis of this awareness, he saw himself as forced to interfere incessantly, entreating or castigating, warning or threatening. Whether writing to a father and mother who tried to prevent their son from entering Clairvaux or to a prince who prevented the introduction of regular canons at a cathedral, it was the cause of reform that drove him on, and in his eyes this was always the business of God. This conviction turned him into a terrible enemy; he was motivated by a cause about whose greatness he could entertain no doubt. This made his indignation against all enemies of reform quite uncontrollable, irrespective of the importance of the matter. When in his letters he hurled curses against the blasphemous, showing no consideration for the individual's reputation, he was in the power of the same passion as had tortured his body and was continually devouring his soul. This man, who had said of the love of God that it was without limit (*sine mensura*), also recognized no limits whatever in his wrath against those who were opposed to God's – and his – cause. It is true that he sometimes encountered criticism for his interference in everything that concerned the Church – on one occasion he even had to accept an unequivocal reprimand from the Curia in Rome – but in the long run neither institutions nor individuals appear to have been able to withstand the enormous power that flowed from him. Praised for his saintly life, admired for his miracles, loved for his zeal, this monk reigned from his monastery over Christendom and its spiritual and worldly rulers.

This became notably apparent from 1130 onwards. Until then Bernard had been mostly concerned with the cause of reform in France itself, but from now on he was thrown into high politics. In 1130 Pope Honorius II died, and in the election of his successor divisions within the body of cardinals produced two rival popes. In both cases the election was carried out in a manner contrary to the canonical regulations. A minority of cardinals under the protection of the Frangipani appointed Innocent II, but the remaining cardinals would not submit to this *coup* and elected instead Peter Leonis (the leader of the most powerful of the local families, the Pierleoni) who adopted the name of Anacletus II. The question now was: whom should Christianity acknowledge as the true pope? Anacletus soon gained the upper hand in Rome and Italy, and Innocent fled to France. As a result of Bernard's intervention, a council in which the king and the great nobles took part gathered around Innocent. The Pope's cause now became Bernard's most important task in the following years. With his usual energy and zeal he took it upon himself to bring the schism to an end. On three occasions, in 1132, 1134–35 and 1137–38, he was in Italy, and he also travelled to Germany as a member of the Pope's retinue. His participation in high politics did not prevent his continuing the pursuit of his true goal; from Germany and from Italy he brought home parties of the converted to Clairvaux. Similarly, his presence in those countries naturally promoted the cause of the Order by the foundation of new monasteries. It is clear that during these years he became closely attached to the pope for whose legitimacy he was fighting so actively and so successfully. In 1138, after the death of Anacletus II, Bernard was instrumental in overcoming the last resistance to Innocent in Italy to such good effect that it was possible for Innocent to take up permanent residence in Rome with an easy mind. Bernard did not return home empty-handed; the Pope's deep gratitude and boundless confidence went with him. He was soon to need both in his fight against Abelard!

So it came about that the very man who had, with greater force than any before him, called the intellectual *élite* of his time to leave the world for a life of poverty and seclusion, began to encroach upon the affairs of the world in many ways. Politics and social morality, science and art, economics and Church leadership, in short all the important areas of social life, became the objects of his activity. But in all this he was still working towards one and the same goal. Bernard was sensible of no contradiction between this versatile activity and the goal he had striven for since his young days in the monastery: to experience true reality in God's presence. He had found the criterion for all he undertook in his lonely cloister cell. He was unable to consider the various fields of intellectual and social life as having more or less their own independent validity, as we would naturally do. He had no 'interest' in science and art as 'worldly' means of expression. Indeed, he had no such 'interests' at all; on the contrary, he found it outrageous to have any. He therefore never considered his standpoint in any matter as being simply a reasonable alternative to the concept he was fighting against, but as 'truth' in opposition to a falsification of life. When he became involved in a theological dispute, it was for him not a question of putting forward a better idea but of fighting as a 'defender of the Faith' against the enemies of Christ. Bernard concerned himself with the spiritual life as he had personally experienced it, even on occasions when, in a more worldly fashion, he pulled strings to have an episcopal seat filled by his nominee. In our eyes, he allowed himself to become involved in many matters not directly within the field of 'religion'. In his eyes, it was the life of solitude in the monastery, of prayer and meditation, that made him aware of the full claims of 'religion', and hence made him encroach upon the life of the world. His life therefore became an incessant double movement: from the silence of monastic life with the brothers at Clairvaux, to action outside, and then back again. In all he undertook his final goal was ever to urge others to undergo the experience that to him was life itself, the unity of love in God. Poverty and solitude – in short, that asceticism which alone can create the abstraction from the world that is the essence of humility – he believed to be the absolute prerequisites for this unity. As a consequence, everything that to his mind stood in the way of this reformed life of the body and the spirit had to be pushed aside, but in the way he went about this he often displayed very little forbearance.

Before we attempt to assess Bernard's purpose and the efforts he made to promote it, we must take a closer look at the basic viewpoint that characterized everything he did. If he is judged solely on the basis of his outward activities, we run the risk of making the task far too easy for ourselves. To any follower of present day cultural prophets, it would be very simple on the basis of the foregoing to categorize him. But it would be wrong to believe that his life and activity can be rejected as an expression of '*dickste Mönchdummheit*', as Schiller wrote to Goethe. On the contrary, his thought is of a rare compactness and consistency. This is not to imply that he is systematic; Bernard produced no philosophical and theological systems in his treatises. By far the greater part of his not very numerous nor comprehensive writings, if lumped together in the old-fashioned way, would probably be classified as 'devotional works'. They are in part sermons given at Clairvaux, including the famous series on the Song of Songs, and in part lesser treatises, almost all concerned with monastic life and often written on request. But in these scattered works – which incidentally can and should be supplemented by his numerous letters, many of which are small treatises in themselves – there is a line of thought which careful reading brings out very clearly. It can be difficult to read him, for unlike the scholastics he has no defined philosophical terminology, but he makes use of a richly varied imagery. He is a distinguished stylist who, as Etienne Gilson, the French historian of the Middle Ages, has pointed out, left it too late in dissociating himself from worldly culture. He was already deeply influenced by classical literature and, when he left the world and its ways behind him, he could not prevent Cicero from slipping in through the monastery gate with him.

It should be made clear that Bernard's profane culture was mainly of a literary character. He had almost no knowledge of the philosophers, Plato and Aristotle. In his eyes they were no more than sophists, and he considered their influence upon higher education to be decidedly harmful. Bernard's theology must be regarded as a meditation upon the mystical experience, and for this he had to look for inspiration to quite different sources. The old accounts of the lives of the Egyptian monastic Fathers were very important, as were also various Christian authors of late Antiquity such as Maximus Confessor (580–662) and John Cassian (c. 360–430/35). In general, it is characteristic of Bernard's attitude that all the elements in his thought are traditional, although the synthesis claims to be original. All theological 'novelties' were an abomination to him. The doctrine had been established and expressed conclusively in the thought of the Church Fathers, above all Augustine. For Bernard, it was only a matter of finding a way of expressing the realization of this in the life of the individual. The monastic tradition itself gave him clear directions: the path of humility is the only road to the love of God, the only true love. His theology is a way of thought along these lines, formalized by an outstanding intellect and undergone as a personal religious experience.

But why, for Bernard, is love of God the only true love? Because it springs from the knowledge of God, which for its part is necessary to man's full knowledge of himself. By seeking to know himself, man becomes aware of his own dignity, of the free will which raises him above the beasts and sets him in a position to rule over them. But, Bernard believes, this knowledge leads us astray if it is not followed by something more. 'It is therefore necessary that you know both things: what you are and what you are not in your own right.' If man does not recognize his dignity, he has none, and he can be considered as no more than a beast. But if he recognizes his dignity without realizing from whence it came it becomes a false dignity. Knowledge of God therefore belongs to true self-knowledge, and from this follows, as already indicated, the demand to love God as the source of the dignity of man. In Bernard's opinion, every person can and should realize all this for himself. Love of God – total love – is for him simply the normal condition of man from which he has been displaced by the Fall. This whole sequence of thought is of course well known in Church tradition. Augustine also had strongly insisted that knowledge of God and of oneself are two sides of the same coin. Before continuing, it is perhaps appropriate to point out here that it was this sequence of thought, originally found in Augustine's Confessions, which shattered the unity of intellectual and rational assumptions that characterized the world of Antiquity. If man's actual being depends entirely upon his relationship to God (that is to say, the infinite; that which does not allow itself to be dominated by and subordinated to the reason of man), then man is no longer the supreme rational being who is only impeded to some small extent by a few sensual desires. Man is in fact only on the verge of freedom, and it is here, in this borderland of what we would now call the conscious and subconscious, that he discovers the essential contradiction in his being, and comes up against the basic problems of his nature and existence. A whole system of psychology owes its existence to these Christian writers; a psychology that tries to penetrate the secret of man's essence, a secret that consists not only in man's relationship to his habits and desires but to his own self. In this matter of the interdependence of God-knowledge and self-knowledge, the 'inactuality' of man becomes evident, but at the same time *history*, the category of time, emerges as the decisive human dimension. In his encounter with the infinite, man becomes conscious of his purpose and destiny, and in consequence he finds or fails to find in this encounter his 'actuality'. It may well be said that the perspectives of this problem have determined our cultural and intellectual environment since that time, not only within the framework of the Church but in a system of cognition, of self-awareness and examination, that retains its character even where all reference to God has become stilled. This is clearly to be seen in much modern literature; in this respect, an author such as Albert Camus is the genuine heir to Augustine and Bernard.

In the case of Bernard also, this sequence of thought leads to a psychological penetration in depth that has preserved its quality to a surprising extent. Although love of God is of a purely spiritual nature, Bernard finds that it begins with a love of the 'flesh'. Man is bound to his physical needs, and he cannot look beyond this until he reaches adulthood. This is natural and right, but since the Fall it has become a serious obstacle. Man is now motivated by desire, *cupiditas*, which is a corruption of nature. As a consequence, all values have been inverted. But even in this condition there is something that reminds us of man's noble nature: desire never rests, because man, God's creation, can rest only in the possession of the eternally good. From likeness to God to unlikeness, from paradise to hell, from God to the Devil, this is man's situation. The question now is whether this is incurable. To answer this, Bernard explains man's original circumstances in more detail: man created in the image of God.

He sees the God-image as notably evident in human will; that is to say, freedom. According to Bernard, man retains freedom in the sense of voluntariness; that is, it is part of the inalienable nature of the will that it cannot be forced to consent to or to reject an act. It is in this freedom that the nobility of man consists. On the other hand, man has lost the true likeness to God that consists of the ability to choose between good and evil, as well as in the strength to do what he has chosen to do. Through sin, will has become wilfulness, which is no more than intellectual ruin – man's desire to follow his own purpose, *consilium proprium*. Man is consequently led into finding pleasure in himself and his own righteousness instead of in God and his righteousness. *Consilium proprium* is therefore idolatry in the final analysis: man's adoration of himself in revolt against God. Bernard sees in this the origin of evil; by preferring himself to God, reason has perverted man's ability to find pleasure only in the good, and has led his will astray.

But by losing his likeness to God – and this is the link that leads back to the starting point – man has also lost his likeness to himself. The question then remains: how can likeness to God be recovered? In this way Bernard arrives at a point that leads directly to the monastic life: it is first necessary for self-will to die. This however has its origin in *consilium proprium*; consequently reason must first submit itself to truth, which is to be found in Faith. Reason being in this way clarified, *consilium proprium* is eliminated so that the will can once more open itself to love, and likeness to God can – little by little – radiate from the soul. It is a long road, but the remedy is sure. Bernard does not conceal that it is best followed in the monasteries, and among these best of all in the Cistercian Order.

Let us now look at this road. To the Cistercians it was concerned with the re-creation of the Christian life following the

Benedictine rule. This is to be learned in the monastic school, which is deliberately contrasted with the contemporary schools in the cathedral towns. The object here is not to learn in order to know – in Bernard's eyes this was precisely Abelard's mistake, as we shall see – but salvation, that is to say the acquisition of that love which is the pre-condition of the true Christian life. The knowledge that leads to this is not that of the philosophers but that taught in the School of Christ. It is a matter of learning the most important of all the 'arts': how to live. The master is Christ Himself, whose 'subject' is love itself, but there are also other masters: fear of God, respect for the rule and a life of penitence. The monastery is the school of love.

The first step along the road is to realize one's unlikeness to God and to act accordingly. This is why the Cistercians begin by killing false love by hard asceticism; this is the price of the freedom that must be won. Life does not consist of asceticism, but it is a necessary condition for that asceticism of thought which is the object in view. To learn to know oneself is now to recognize oneself as a fallen sinner; that is to say, to learn humility, *humilitas*. Humility leads to love of those who condemn their wretchedness, who judge themselves as God judges them, and who, to prove this, punish themselves by mortifying the flesh. In this way they have unified their will with God's will, and it becomes revealed that even humility is love.

But this is only the feeble beginning. To know oneself is to know the truth, also concerning one's neighbour. This is not to say that the monk is to pass judgement on him; on the contrary, he is in this way awakened to suffer with his neighbour. This is manifested in the charity the Order stresses. Much of Bernard's indignation against rich monasteries arises from their use to buy ornaments, etcetera of money which might have been given to the poor. Man has a right only to what is absolutely necessary to sustain the body. But the monk, in realizing this, renounces his self-will and discovers the 'common will', *voluntas communis*, which is love. As yet, however, only a 'physical' love is concerned, which is expressed as a will towards social justice. What is more important is that the extension of self-knowledge to cover everyone also implies that Jesus comes into view. This new 'physical' love is also concerned with Jesus as a *man*. In

Bernard's mysticism, this is the point for meditation upon Jesus' earthly life. Because of man's limitation to what is sensible, love of the Saviour also begins with love of the flesh, that is to say the contemplation of His person, life, death and resurrection. Slowly now the love begins to grow that prepares man for full unity with the will of God, the experience that Bernard in the language of the hymn refers to as 'the bridegroom's visit'.

Through continuous mortification and meditation on the person of Jesus, the nature of the soul is purified and converted; that is to say love, which signifies the freeing of the will from the slavery of sin, increasingly takes shape in the soul so that the original likeness to God comes into view. Instead of laying down his own law, man is now free and is spontaneously subjected to God's law, which is the Holy Spirit, the mutual love of the Father and the Son. Humility through contemplation of Jesus' earthly life is the first stage, purification through love is the second. The third and last stage is the union with God in His divine sublimity. This comes to pass through what Bernard refers to as *raptus* or *excessus*, the ecstatic experience, 'the bridegroom's kiss'. In this union of the soul with God, the contrast between love of God and self-love has disappeared. When likeness to God has been re-created, to love oneself is the same as loving this likeness to God, and consists in the very love of God for God's own sake. Consequently, in the same way as the love God has for us is nothing other than the love He has for Himself, so is the love we have for ourselves nothing other than the love we have for God. On this basis it becomes comprehensible that the life of love is all an endeavour towards the mystical union with God: it is indeed the likeness to God that we love in ourselves, and similarly this is what God loves in us. Therefore, the likeness must include the longing for unity with God. Viewed in this light, mysticism in Bernard's view is not confined to a special personal experience but is the goal of the complete Christian life as translated into action in the cloister.

Bernard's mysticism is devoid of all pantheism. Any thought of substantial integration between God and the soul is excluded. Bernard certainly speaks of 'making divine' the soul, but he means by this a conformity of wills, not a fusing together of them. If one objects that the elimination of man's self-will leads to the negation of man's self, Bernard can easily refute such an accusation. The contrary is in fact the case; it is precisely through the abolition of self-will that man regains his true nature, which is to be like unto God in the unity of love. Therefore, the more the will of man conforms to that of God, the more he becomes himself. It might be said, then, that man's awareness of the image of God in man is at the centre of Bernard's theology. The description of man's way out of perversion and back to God, that is to say to love, is a description of how man becomes once again what he was destined to be. Mysticism, the individual concentration on the contemplation of God, is therefore not in principle a particular vocation for a specially selected few, although it may well have been so in practice and often still is. Bernard himself fully realizes that what he considers to be pure 'disinterested' love can never become an enduring condition, but is reserved for select moments of ecstasy. He therefore does not become a quietist; the demands of active life have their necessary place also.

Whatever we may think of this, we are forced to admit that it is consistently thought out from beginning to end. This line of thought also explains why Bernard was forced to react vehemently against all intellectual activity that appeared to him to lead away from the path of love, even if only by not furthering the journey along it. Therefore, all his meddling in matters outside the monastery walls sprang not from any independent interest on his part but rather from a fear that these matters might take on an independent significance for others, and thereby create obstacles to 'the one thing necessary'. Bernard's 'cultural policy' is therefore quite unequivocal, and there is no need for him to argue step by step since everything is predetermined. It would of course be foolish to assess this on the basis of our secularized conception of culture. Anything of that nature was in any case forbidden in the times he lived in. But although the truth and universal dominance of the Christian revelation was accepted even among philosophers and artists, this did not mean that Bernard's conception of the Christian life was the only conceivable one. In practice, of course, this was certainly not so; ambition and vanity are no modern inventions. But in theory also the same was true; it was in fact in Bernard's own lifetime that a humanistic absorption with man and his world broke through traditional attitudes. This was not looked upon as an enemy of Christianity, which indeed it was not, but it stood in striking contrast to the attitude of Bernard and his associates in the reform movement, and it was in this way that he came to represent traditionalism in the struggle against the new thought. But it is proof of the enormous forces contained in the monastic movement of the Western world that the same monks who defended themselves by summoning up all the courage of the old authorities against what they considered to be 'perverse novelties' were able to give new strength and direction to monasticism through their efforts for reform. Of these monks, Bernard was the greatest. In his thought, tradition was converted into an original achievement that provided inspiration for generations to come. It is part of the greatness of this work that Bernard, by his – in principle – anti-humanistic thought, contributed to the acquisition of new knowledge for the Europe whose progress he sought to arrest. His penetrating analyses contributed appreciably to the unceasing new formulations of the old question: what is man?

Although Bernard's conception of Christianity clarifies his views on culture and politics, it does not of course provide an excuse for all his acts. Apart from this, questions might well be asked concerning his conception of the Christian life: is it a conception of the Christian life at all? Were the ideals and practices of the Cistercian Order a fulfilment of the life of the first Church? What has been said in this chapter will not provide an answer, and much of any answer that is provided will depend upon our assessment of the contest about to be described. It was our intention here to explain as far as possible Bernard's attitude and motives. He will have need of all the understanding he can call upon!

CHAPTER 7

The Attack

It is easy to imagine the happiness Abelard would have found when he resumed teaching in Paris in 1136. After all the years of disappointment and adversity he was once more in his true element. What triumph he must have enjoyed to find he still possessed the old power over his listeners! The great influx to his lectures would have revived the transcription of his books. Arising from the reports of the happenings in Paris, these books would have undergone a renaissance also in the distant parts of the country, indeed far beyond the frontiers of France. It is possible that the *Theologia*, or at any rate part of it, was written at the Paraclete as early as the beginning of the 1120s, but in any case it was the furore surrounding Abelard's resumed teaching that first gave it a real circulation. It would otherwise be incomprehensible that before this time the work should have caused no anxiety among the more traditionally minded.[1] John of Salisbury, to whom we are indebted for the information that it was in 1136 that Abelard returned to Paris, tells that he soon left again.[2] We are unable to follow his movements in the following years, but there is reason to believe that he was not absent for long. The whole sequence of events that led to the Synod of Sens and Abelard's condemnation in 1140 would have no explanation if we did not assume that he continued his teaching activities. This of course is not to suggest that there were no intervals. In any event, it is certain that he occupied a dominant position in the academic world, and particularly in Paris, in the years after 1136.

But he was not allowed to enjoy this new triumph for long. A copy of his *Theologia* travelled as far as the remote Cistercian monastery of Signy, where it came into the hands of the former Benedictine abbot and Bernard's close friend, William of St Thierry. His curiosity was aroused by the strange title, and he immersed himself in the reading of the book. The contents horrified him, and he immediately set about writing a treatise directed against Abelard.[3] This he sent with a letter to Bernard and to the papal legate in France, Bishop Geoffrey of Chartres.[4] We do not know precisely when this letter was written, but from Bernard's reply it appears that Easter was approaching. We must assume from this that Bernard's letter was written early in the year. As Bernard had returned home in 1138 after a very long absence abroad, there is reason to believe that William approached him at the beginning of 1139.[5] We have no information of Geoffrey of Chartres' reaction to this approach, but we do know that Bernard was prepared thoroughly to investigate the matter. In this way arose the situation that was soon to develop into a bitter struggle between him and Abelard. But before we go on to follow the events, let us examine the degree to which the conflicting parties knew each other at this time.

In the account of his period at the Paraclete in the 1120s, Abelard writes that his old rivals now succeeded in stirring up against him some new apostles of great importance in the eyes of the world. Of these he writes: '... one of them was conceited enough to assert that he had aroused the regular canons, the other the monks, to new life.'[6] It is generally agreed that the 'apostles' he had in mind were Norbert of Xanten, the founder of the Premonstratensian congregation, and Bernard of Clairvaux. In Norbert's case there is scarcely any doubt.[7] Bernard's activity in the restoration of monastic discipline was so well known and, incidentally, without parallel at the time that he is naturally taken to be the other.[8] If this is correct, Abelard had recognized Bernard as a threat even while still at the Paraclete. In his treatise *On Baptism*, written in about 1125, Bernard replies to some questions concerning the views of a master whose identity he says he does not know.[9] The teaching of this man, whom Bernard opposes very strongly, is to the effect that ignorance excuses all sin. This viewpoint is quoted in a manner corresponding precisely to Abelard's teaching in the *Ethica*; if he is not the person aimed at, it must be one of his disciples. There is some reason to believe that this treatise of Bernard's was the cause of Abelard's fear of him, but it is impossible to be certain about this.

Another connection between the two parties concerns the Paraclete after it was taken over by Heloïse. A letter from Abelard to Bernard shows that the latter, at the request of Heloïse, had paid a visit to the Paraclete, where he had been satisfied with all he saw except for one liturgical detail, of which Abelard was the originator. The letter is quite friendly, but on the facts of the matter Abelard defends himself without giving an inch.[10] This consequently gives us no indication of the relationship between them. It might perhaps be said that the visit to Heloïse must presuppose a good relationship, since she would scarcely receive a man who harboured hostile feelings towards Abelard.[11] On the other hand, it is equally possible that the invitation to Bernard was seen as a purely tactical move – a wish to offer him an opportunity to convince himself that all was according to rule. It is impossible in all this to go beyond supposition. Only one thing is certain: on January 20, 1131, both Abelard and Bernard were staying at the monastery of Morigny on the occasion of the visit of Pope Innocent II. Abelard had presented himself to request that a papal legate be sent to his monastery with a view to its reform.[12] As Bernard belonged to the close circle around the Pope, he would have come to know Abelard personally on this occasion, even if he had not met him earlier. It is therefore at least certain they were acquainted. Nor can there be any doubt that Bernard would have heard of Abelard's resumed activity in Paris after 1136, but it is of course possible that he had no detailed information about it. He was, indeed, resident in Italy for long periods up to the end of 1138 in connection with the Roman schism.

In his letter to Bernard and Geoffrey of Chartres, William of St Thierry says that he had loved Abelard. If this is not empty rhetoric, it must be a reference to an earlier friendship, and J. M. Dechanet has examined this question in an article. On the basis of the chronology in the lives of the two men, he arrives at the conclusion that the friendship must belong to a period around 1112 or 1113 when they were both studying under Anselm of Laon. Dechanet sets out to prove that there was in fact a student relationship between William and Abelard during that period. Various features distinguishing William from his friends, for example Bernard, he seeks to trace back to Abelard's influence. There is, in fact, no certainty here either, but Dechanet has at least shown it to be probable that the two men knew one another.[13]

Finally, in the case of Geoffrey of Chartres, his feelings towards Abelard had long been friendly. It was he who at the Council of Soissons had tried in vain to save him from an unjust conviction. Meanwhile however he had become a friend of Bernard. But this is scarcely a good reason for William to send his letter and thesis to Geoffrey also, who was at the time the papal legate in France, and therefore in any event the representative of the highest Church authority. William says in his letter that he has chosen to approach Bernard and Geoffrey precisely because Abelard would fear *them*. It is possible that he had Geoffrey in mind particularly because of his official position, even though Bernard's reputation – no less than his influence – could well make him a formidable opponent.

William's letter goes straight to the point, in very disturbed language. The faith is in danger, and as all others are silent he will speak. He is deeply sad, but even so it must be said: Peter Abelard once again teaches and writes about new things. His books are widely broadcast, even beyond the Alps. They are held in esteem even by the Curia in Rome. Action must therefore be taken for the sake of the Church. William says he came upon Abelard's *Theologia* by accident, because the title made him curious. He then adds: '... but there were two books whose contents were almost the same, except that there was rather more in the one and rather less in the other.' While he was reading, he made notes which he encloses – that is, the treatise directed against Abelard. To give more emphasis to the danger of these books, which are full of 'new things' – unheard of opinions invented by Abelard himself – William points out that all the old masters are dead, and teaching is left almost to

Abelard alone. In other words: there is no one there to stop him.[14]

In this letter, we already come across some of the points that, in the later struggle, Abelard's opponents used against him with decisive effect. First, the emphasis on the fact that he taught 'new things'. The matter-of-course way this is produced as a proof of guilt is a very characteristic feature of their attitude. It is not merely a manifestation of reluctance to see established positions disputed, nor simply a matter of that normal torpidity which can at any time arouse aversion to what is new; we should not be too hasty in acquitting our own times of this, relegating it entirely to a comfortably remote past. It is of course possible that such motives may have played their part, but first and foremost a point of principle was concerned: quite simply, the Fathers, that is to say the approved orthodox tradition, had said all that was necessary. To introduce new presentations of problems is therefore the same as being on the way to heresy. The onlooker might well say that Church traditionalism hated anyone who was not an imitator; the original is suspicious in itself. It is weighty proof of the extent and strength of this attitude that so much stress was laid upon the fact that Abelard taught new things.

The other point which there is reason to underline in the letter is of a more practical nature: the emphasis on Abelard's wide influence, both oral and written, which can be expected to have the most disastrous consequences for the Church. It is bad enough in itself that he teaches new things, but the worst is that so many listen to him. This consideration takes the matter beyond the purely dogmatic level and directly into ecclesiastical politics.

William's letter was accompanied by a refutation of Abelard set out in thirteen points. As a basis, William uses the *Theologia* and the other book he refers to which is said to have had almost the same content. But he denies any knowledge of *Sic et Non* and the *Ethica*. The question is, what other book can he have drawn upon? It is probably the work that Bernard also uses later, bearing the title *The Book of the Sentences*. It was not written by Abelard but by one of his pupils.[15] William's refutation would have given Bernard a good idea of its content, and it was certainly extensively used by Bernard when he himself later set out to write a treatise directed against Abelard. In his reply to William's appeal, Bernard acknowledges the seriousness of the matter but also admits that he has only had time quickly to run through William's treatise. As he dare not trust his own judgment in such an important matter,[16] he suggests that he should meet William after Easter. Finally, he asks William to show understanding of his previous silence in this matter as hitherto he has been ignorant of most of it, indeed of almost all of it.[17]

Although we have no information about this, it must be assumed that the proposed meeting in fact took place, and that at this meeting Bernard became convinced of the need to intervene. In the first instance he tried to negotiate a settlement through a meeting with Abelard. There is reason to believe that the discussions were carried on in a friendly atmosphere,[18] and it is very probable that Abelard was genuinely prepared for peace. The memory of his humiliation at Soissons had burnt deep into his sensitive nature, and he can certainly have had no urge to expose himself once again to an inquisition. We do not know to what extent Abelard submitted to Bernard's demands during this conversation with him,[19] but it is conceivable that his pupils felt they were not themselves bound by any subjection on the part of the master, and consequently persisted in the points of view that had horrified Bernard.[20] This may have convinced the abbot that more effective measures were necessary, and it was of course a matter not only of stopping Abelard but also of bringing his destructive influence to a halt. Like the politician he was, Bernard therefore set out to take counter-measures. This he did in various ways.

According to Abelard, Bernard first approached the Archbishop of Sens, since the diocese of Paris was part of his ecclesiastical province.[21] As this led to nothing, he then approached the Bishop of Paris, Abelard's rightful authority. Bernard probably tried to persuade the bishop to intervene, and he was given permission to preach to the students in Paris himself. It appears that the bishop was reluctant to become involved, but by giving permission to Bernard to preach he was taking the side of Bernard, who was certainly able to make good use of the opportunity offered. His sermon contains a remarkably sharp attack on Abelard, for although he mentions no names, there could have been no doubt at whom he was aiming.[22] This can have had no good effect upon his relations with Abelard; it was an undisguised attempt to take his students away from him – a frontal attack upon his reputation and honour as a master. However reasonable this action may have been from Bernard's viewpoint, it is not surprising that, instead of causing Abelard to retract or correct his teaching, it gave him other matters to consider. It was probably at about the time of these events that he published the fourth edition of the *Theologia*, in which he takes some notice of William's criticism, although persisting in his teaching in all its essentials.[23]

It was perhaps the knowledge of this which caused Bernard to take the final step: an approach to Rome. In spite of a certain amount of sympathy from the Bishop of Paris, his efforts had so far shown no progress. An additional reason to approach the pope and the cardinals may also have been his and William's unease that Abelard might have friends and influence at Rome also. With this begins the flood of letters from Clairvaux to Rome, and with one of these was enclosed Bernard's treatise against Abelard's heresy. A whole series of letters exists whose dates are unfortunately uncertain in many cases. We are therefore reduced to trying to date them on the basis of their contents and in relation to the events whose sequence is known. The following is certain: after Bernard had made his accusation against Abelard to the pope, Abelard, who had probably learned almost immediately of the contents of Bernard's treatise, published the fifth and last edition of the *Theologia* in which he sets out his views on the treatise, in general adhering to his previous teaching. In addition he persuaded the Archbishop of Sens to arrange a meeting between him and Bernard on June 3, 1140. This meeting, through Bernard's efforts, was transformed into a synod which condemned nineteen of Abelard's propositions. However, the synod did not condemn his person because he appealed from there to Rome. Abelard now prepared to set out for Rome to conduct his own case, but before he got very far the Pope's condemnation supervened. The matter was now concluded; Abelard yielded to the Pope's decision and was reconciled with the Church and with Bernard. Soon after, in 1142, he died.

The sequence of events, briefly described here so that we may understand more readily the following account, is full of dramatic details whose relationship one with another we are obliged to reconstruct. First we shall describe the apparent chain of events. Then, at the end of this chapter, we shall deal in rather more detail with the content of Bernard's criticism.

Apart from the treatise directed against Abelard, Bernard's collection of letters includes two more letters to Pope Innocent II concerning Abelard; ep. 189 and 330. The treatise, ep. 190, belongs to the period before the Synod of Sens. Ep. 189 is Bernard's account of the synod and it can thereby be dated; it was probably written on the same day as the synod, or on the subsequent day. Ep. 330 remains, which is strikingly similar to ep. 189, but contains no account of the events at Sens. It is probably a draft for ep. 189.[24] The remaining letters are in most cases directed to cardinals. One is aimed at the cardinals and bishops of the Curia in general, and one is to an abbot in Italy at the time. We can place with full certainty only those letters which, because of their content, must belong to the period after the synod. These we can leave aside for the moment. Some however remain that are more difficult to place; were they dispatched before or after the synod? It is indeed true that, apart from the treatise sent to the pope, we can say of none of the letters that it is *impossible* for them to have been written after the synod. The older construction, which usually assigns all the letters to that period, cannot therefore be completely rejected. But several of these letters can be explained more naturally if their purpose was to provoke a Roman initiative in the matter of Abelard at a time when Bernard did not yet know that he would be summoned to Sens. A minute examination of the letters shows that the whole of this body of material is linked. The same phrases reappear again and again, but often in new contexts. This would of course be most readily explained if they were all written at the same time, but on the other hand there is no reason why Bernard should not have repeated himself in a number of letters, as he did on numerous other occasions. Further, we must take into account the possibility that some of the letters may have been drafted before the synod but not dispatched until after it had been held.

If a comparison is made between the letters as a whole, it is conspicuous that the letters giving the information that Abelard is about to come to Rome, and which can therefore be dated after the synod, do not give a particularly detailed description of Abelard's person and teaching, whereas those letters giving no information about his journey have many features in common, not only in their stern condemnation of Abelard's person but also in their description of his teaching. It is justifiable to ask, as does the German scholar Arno Borst, why Bernard in these letters should compare Abelard with Arius, Pelagius and Nestorius (the heretics of the early Church) if his addressees had in front of them, when they received the letters, a list of Abelard's condemned propositions. But such comparisons make good sense if the object was to stir Rome into action. On the basis of this argument there is good reason to assign a number of the letters to the period before the synod.[25] The group of letters here referred to differs not only from those we can with certainty assign to the period after the synod, but also from the letter to the pope that accompanied the treatise and from the letter to the cardinals and bishops of the Curia. These two letters are strictly objective, in that they are concerned only with the supposedly heretical in Abelard's writings and with the problem of how to silence him. The other letters are however coloured by a fury that must be the result of some new experience. Against the background of these considerations, it should now be possible to give a reasonable account of the developments.

After the unsuccessful approaches to Sens and Paris, only Rome remained. Bernard therefore wrote to the pope with a request for intervention against Abelard. He gave his detailed reasons for this request, on the one hand in the accompanying treatise, which attacked in particular Abelard's teaching on the Trinity and on the Atonement, and on the other in the accompanying list of heretical propositions, *capitula*, in Abelard's books.[26] In support of this request, he wrote, perhaps at the same time, a letter to the cardinals in which he demonstrates the responsibility of the Roman Church towards its believers. Hur and Aaron. who supported Moses' hands in the desert battle

against Amalek, are likened to the zeal and authority of the
Roman Church. Bernard therefore considers himself justified in
appealing to the cardinals when the faith is attacked and Christ
insulted. He gives a brief characterization of Abelard's theological activity, and invites the cardinals to read his works.[27]
The letter ends with an injunction that they should act, if
reading Abelard's works should cause them the same consterna-
tion as Bernard has himself experienced.

By these approaches, Bernard had done all he could to put a
stop to Abelard, but without result. The question remains, what
can have made him send a series of letters to individual members
of the Curia, bearing in mind that the tone of each of these
letters is completely different? It would of course be most natural
to assume that the knowledge of Abelard's reply in the fifth
edition of the *Theologia* to Bernard's attack had caused Bernard
to abandon all discretion. As has recently been said, these new
letters are written 'with consummate diplomatic skill'.[28] Guy of
Castello, known to be a friend of Abelard, was a dangerous
man. The letter to him is remarkably subdued in its tone. Even
so, Abelard is associated in it with the usual heretics of the early
Church. We learn that he teaches 'profane new things', and
that he claims to know everything, while it would be better for
him if he knew himself. It is not Bernard who accuses him, the
letter reads, but his own book. The main point of the letter is
however its addressee: Bernard will not believe of Guy – no
matter what others say – that he stretches his friendship so far
that he even comes to love the errors of his friend. 'Certain
people judge first and learn later, but I do not wish to judge
whether the drink is sweet or bitter before I have tasted it.'
Bernard has no wish to believe anything bad of Guy, since a
friendship that also embraces errors would be earthly, animal,
indeed devilish. Perhaps therefore it would be better for the
Cardinal, as well as for the Church and for Abelard, if his
(Abelard's) mouth were to be closed; this mouth so full of
condemnation, bitterness and deceit.[29] In this way Bernard hoped
to neutralize the goodwill Abelard enjoyed with the Curia.

He writes in quite a different manner to the other cardinals,
Ivo, Stephen and Gregory. They are all men he can rely upon,
and he can therefore express freely what is in his heart. He gives

vent here to all his indignation. The three letters are introduced with unrestrained descriptions of Abelard's person: he is a monk without rule, a prelate without sense of responsibility,[30] an abbot without discipline,[31] outwardly a John but inwardly a Herod;[32] he argues with boys and consorts with women,[33] he is a questionable character who has only name and habit in common with a monk.[34] Following this character sketch, Bernard adds in one of the letters: 'But what has this to do with me? Each must bear his own burden.'[35] This however does not prevent his writing as he does. Apart from this, Abelard is described as a persecutor of the Church and an enemy of the Cross of Christ.[36] He corrupts the faith and makes changes as the whim takes him.[37] Bernard sees him as a regenerator of the heretics of old, since in all three letters he brings in Arius, Pelagius and Nestorius as bogy-men. But the rage is directed towards the nature of Abelard's theology – towards his whole band of disciples; he tries to penetrate the secrets of God; he exceeds the limits set by the Fathers; there is nothing in heaven nor on earth he does not know, except himself.[38] Bernard reminds them that Abelard has already been condemned at Soissons, but adds that he is like a hydra that grows seven new heads as soon as one is cut off.[39] In different form, all three letters end with requests for intervention.

The letter to an unknown abbot has a similar content.[40] All these letters bear strong witness to Bernard's intention to put an end to his enemy. One must admire his skill in repeating his finely elaborated attack with constant variation. The components are stereotyped, but repeatedly set within new frameworks adapted to the individual addressees. Abelard's influence with the Curia, witnessed to by both William and Bernard, must certainly have been strong if all this could not bring about the desired result. In spite of his unparalleled energy and inventiveness, Bernard achieved nothing by his immense effort. Circumstances that he could not have foreseen and whose possibilities he could not immediately assess were to give him the opportunity he lacked.

Before we follow the further course of events, we shall stop for a moment to seek an answer to the question: what was it that made Bernard so embittered towards Abelard and all his activities? This can of course be answered to some extent from the letters referred to above, but they tell us almost more about the degree of Bernard's rage. Personal bitterness colours his statements to such an extent that it is difficult on their basis alone to know for certain what it was all about. The treatise against Abelard is in this respect far more informative. Whereas William of St Thierry in his refutation deals with very many points, almost all of which were revived in the list of Abelard's heresies at the Synod of Sens, Bernard mentions most of these matters only in passing, and otherwise concentrates upon the teaching on the Trinity and on atonement. As already pointed out, his criticism is primarily directed against Abelard's actual method of dealing with theology. The individual passages in Abelard's works to which he refers directly are to him only a long series of examples of the master's method – in his boundless arrogance – of treating what is holy in the most ungodly and impudent manner. Abelard's intention – *to understand* Revelation – is for Bernard proof that Abelard wishes to use reason to penetrate the secrets of God. Such a thing is not permissible: we are permitted only to mark the effect of God's will and to perceive its beneficial fruit. The following statement is characteristic: 'Why, you ask, did God do by the Blood (that is to say through the death of Christ) what he could do by the Word alone? Ask God himself. It is permitted to me to know that it was so, but why it was so I am not permitted to know.'[41] Bernard consequently is not prepared to recognize any questioning of the reasons for belief, *ratio fidei*. Quite apart from whatever result Abelard arrives at, he has already erred in the manner itself of his questioning.

Bernard describes Abelard's intentions in bitingly sarcastic terms. There is nothing in heaven nor on earth he does not know! He investigates God's majesty and insults the Holy Trinity with his profane similes. He wishes to subject everything to his reason – this other Aristotle who has himself almost become a heathen, as was his exemplar.[42] Abelard adds and subtracts at his own discretion. This 'reckless searcher after God's majesty' has the audacity openly to go against the Fathers.[43] He will believe nothing he cannot understand by his reasoning. Bernard overwhelms him with embittered exclamations: perverse dogmas, profane innovations, blasphemy, impudence, ungodliness, slander! In short, Bernard accuses Abelard of being a rationalist. To ask for causes and reasons, to seek to understand the Trinity, is to insult the faith and to persecute Christ's Church. In one respect it might be said that Bernard saw in Abelard precisely what in our day – from a diametrically opposite valuation – it has sometimes been sought to make of him: a disrespectful advocate of free thought, a kind of enlightening philosopher born six hundred years too early.

This intense aversion to Abelard's theological methods naturally colours also Bernard's comprehension of his teaching. He sees him as a regenerator of old heresies, and also as an inventor of new ones. His attack on Abelard's teaching on the Trinity he concentrated on the images and similes Abelard uses, which Bernard considers to be unemployable – quite apart from the impudence they suggest. He arrives at this result by drawing from the similes conclusions in no way intended by Abelard. Although Abelard points out very clearly what they are similes of, Bernard ignores this limitation and treats them as if they were straight-forward comparisons, in all points congruent with the matter to be explained.[44] The teaching on atonement is subjected to a detailed and thorough investigation in which, stage by stage, Bernard discusses Abelard's draft of the commentary on the Epistle to the Romans. Somewhat absurdly, he sees it as quite an original heresy of Abelard that, in contrast to the Fathers, he will not hear speak of the devil's right over man. We have already seen that Anselm of Canterbury was ahead of Abelard here. As concerns Abelard's teaching, Bernard finds that he has reduced the acts of Christ to no more than an example to be followed.[45]

In view of the close relationship between Bernard and Innocent II, due to a large extent to Bernard's victory over the antipope Anacletus II, one might anticipate that the treatise and the accompanying list of Abelard's heresies would cause the pope to act; but nothing happened. Instead, the heretic persisted and published an edition of the *Theologia* that took Bernard's objections into consideration, but in such a form that there was little in the way of admission of error.[46] But although Abelard's influence with the Curia was still strong enough to prevent any action against him, he was fully aware of the danger inherent in Bernard's attack. The personal bitterness, which was now implacable on both sides, probably also helped to determine his tactics. Now that the matter had become known far and wide, Abelard could see no other way out than the solution he had tried so many times before, and which incidentally was so well suited to his temperament: to fight his way through. He took this decision on the basis of a supreme confidence in his intellectual superiority. Bernard's action convinced him of the necessity to make the dispute, already known everywhere, fully public. The consequence of this was the approach to the Archbishop of Sens.

CHAPTER 8

The Encounter at Sens

The recently published letter from Abelard to his friends and disciples[1] makes it clear that he viewed Bernard's action in the same light as, in his autobiography, he had judged the behaviour of his other enemies – that is, as an expression of envy. He speaks bitterly of Bernard as an old enemy who until this very moment has pretended to be a friend. Bernard had written that the *Theologia* should rather have been called the *Stultilogia* (from *stultus*: foolish), and this appears to have hurt him.[2] It is incidentally apparent from the letter that Abelard had heard of Bernard's approach to the Archbishop of Sens, in the presence of many of his own friends, and he had also heard how Bernard, as he expresses it, had 'belched forth from the depth of his wickedness' in Paris. What is to Bernard the cause of Christ is, in Abelard's eyes nothing more than the spiteful envy of a monk inferior to him in intellect. Abelard finally writes that the Archbishop has now sent Bernard a letter to the effect that, if he wishes to pursue his accusations, Abelard is prepared to reply to his *'capitula'* – that is, his list of suspicious propositions – on the Sunday after Whitsun.[3] These *capitula* would be identical with the list Bernard had sent to the pope.[4] Further, the letter shows that Abelard had not as yet been informed of Bernard's reply, but he asks his friends to come to Sens to stand by him.

The Archbishop of Sens had failed to act as Bernard wished, but he willingly complied with Abelard's appeal. This need not necessarily indicate that he took Abelard's side, but it is certain he must have accepted the role Abelard intended for him – a kind of arbitrator in the discussion – and it is not inconceivable that he may have wished to impose this difficult situation on Bernard. These two had earlier been at loggerheads with one another. One of the most distasteful letters in all Bernard's collection is directed to Henry of Sens.[5] It is true they had become reconciled a short time before, but the high prelate can scarcely have nourished any especially friendly feelings towards Bernard.

Bernard however had no intention at all of appearing. He simply refused.[6] He was honest enough later to admit to the pope that he found a verbal dispute with the famous dialectician not particularly tempting. But he had other reasons more related to principle on which to found his refusal: faith should not be made the subject of dispute; Abelard's heresy is clearly apparent from his books; finally it is a matter for the bishops, and not for Bernard, to judge Abelard.[7] In spite of all these excellent reasons for staying at home, the end result was that Bernard had to change his mind. Abelard did all he could to make it known that he was going to reply to Bernard at Sens, and he invited a great number of people. Bernard however, in his letter to the pope, says that even this could not move him, as he did not care what people said. He also refers to Abelard's activities: 'What he has been writing about me to his disciples I would rather not say.'[8] But in the end he gave in to the advice of his friends, albeit reluctantly; they were afraid that Bernard's failure to appear would enhance Abelard's reputation and give offence to the people there.[9] We may believe Bernard when he says that he gave in only with reluctance, indeed with tears. But when he adds that he came unprepared and unprotected it is not so easy to take him seriously. He had in any case taken care to write a plaintive letter to the bishops, in which he earnestly begs them to appear and to show themselves to be friends, not of him, but of Christ. The Bride of Christ calls them to the forest of heresy where she is in danger of strangulation. The Bridegroom's friends (the bishops) should not betray the Bride of Christ in her misery. He explains why he writes so late in the day by adding that his opponent, in his cunning, has taken care to direct his attack

against the unconcerned and unsuspecting, forcing the unprotected to appear.[10] To say the least, this can only be regarded as
a somewhat one-sided account.

The atmosphere during the period preceding the meeting at
Sens was consequently very sombre, and characterized by the
deepest mutual suspicion, not to say hatred. Both sides sought to
mobilize all their forces. Abelard's letter to his friends and
Bernard's to the bishops here confront one another. Knowing
the background, a comparison between the two letters proves
very enlightening. Personal bitterness is equally strong in both,
and each equally feels that he is the victim of treachery. Yet
though they are alike in their attitudes towards each other and
in their determination to maintain their positions unyieldingly,
their approach to the substance and form of the debate could
scarcely be more different. Abelard pleads only his own cause;
he feels that his honour as a master has been deeply outraged,
and he seeks an opportunity to defend it against the ambush of
envy. His reliance on his own superiority leads him to regard an
opportunity to fight as almost the same as victory. For him it is
all a matter of arguments, and he has no doubt who will have
the best of these! Bernard goes about things in quite a different
way. He pleads – he believes in – not his own cause but that of
God and the Church. In his usual metaphorical style, he urges
the bishops to stand with him against the destroyer. The matter
to hand is, for him, not an academic discussion but a fight
against heresy, the very destruction of life. By using images
from the Song of Songs, by which he lived and breathed, he sees
himself as the personification of the Church in battle with the
dragon – the evil powers that are opposed to God. The disputation, which Abelard desired and considered to be the only just
process, Bernard, from his utterly different point of view, sought
to prevent at any price. All courtesy was forgotten on both
sides. Abelard's only desire was to make Bernard a laughing-
stock in a public debate, and so to silence his enemy. Bernard's
object, on the other hand, was to secure Abelard's conviction for
heresy, and thus to have his books condemned, any further
teaching banned and his influence finally destroyed. The gap
was unbridgeable, and from the outset the battle could scarcely
end in anything but the unequivocal defeat of one of them.

In the period before the meeting at Sens, Abelard acquired a follower unlikely to commend his cause at Rome. This was the Italian priest Arnold of Brescia (1100–1155) who, through his teaching that the Church should renounce all its earthly possessions, had advanced the movement towards the liberation of the Italian towns from the sovereignty of the Church. He came to Paris, where he attached himself to Abelard in his dispute with Bernard, whom Arnold accused of vanity.[11] Another Italian also joined Abelard's camp at this time: the Roman sub-deacon Hyacinth, who without doubt was his disciple. He probably appeared because he had become alarmed by Bernard's plea to Rome – indeed, perhaps he came as a kind of emissary from Abelard's supporters in the Roman Curia. Everything was now ready for the great trial of strength.

The Sunday after Whitsun, 1140, had already been signalled as a day to remember. A display of relics belonging to Sens Cathedral was to be the occasion of great festivities on that very day, and the presence of the king and his court was expected. It followed that the other bishops of the arch-diocese would also be present as far as was possible. It was therefore Abelard's intention to take advantage of these circumstances; the planned festivities were a guarantee that a discussion between him and Bernard would not pass without comment! As a result of Abelard's reaction to Bernard's attack, however, the character of the festivities was entirely changed. It was possibly due to Bernard, whose friends they were, that the Archbishop of Rheims, together with some of his suffragens, made his way to Sens on the second of June, and monks, priests and personalities from the academic and secular worlds flocked to the city from all quarters to be present at the great contest.

After the meeting, Bernard wrote to the pope that he had gone to Sens confidently believing that the inspiration of the Holy Spirit would direct what he was to say, but it should be added that as a precaution he had also made a plan.[12] On the second of June he preached to the people and asked them to pray for Abelard.[13] Later in the day he assembled the bishops for a consultation, and appeared here with a list of Abelard's heresies. In spite of Hyacinth, who would have been present, he succeeded in carrying his point of view. His complaint concerning

Hyacinth to the pope and his chancellor, Cardinal Haimeric, suggests that Hyacinth went so far as to threaten him;[14] but, be that as it may, he persuaded the bishops to support him. Among these were many of his close friends and at least one of Abelard's old enemies, Joscelin of Soisson.

Berengar of Poitier, Abelard's disciple, gives a scurrilous account of the state the bishops were in at the meeting, which is difficult to believe but too amusing to be ignored. He asserts that they were so sleepy from the wine they had taken with their meal that they had great difficulty in following Bernard's exposition. To his question: *damnatis?* (that is to say: do you condemn?), it was, he maintains, difficult for some of the worthy gentlemen to pronounce the word *damnamus* (we condemn). They dropped the first syllable, and so, with *namus* (we are floating or swimming) they unwittingly described their sodden state![15]

Whatever the circumstances may have been, Bernard got what he wanted. By these tactics he had ensured his control of the events of the following day. He had no longer to attack his feared opponent in the face of an impartial audience; he was now the designated prosecutor of a court of inquisition. There can be no doubt that Abelard was informed that the basis for all his assumptions about the form of the proceedings had thereby been destroyed. He of course carefully considered how he should act in this new situation. Informed of Bernard's careful preparations (which as one of Bernard's modern biographers says without a vestige of subtlety 'simplified the public discussions of the synod'[16]), Abelard was fully aware of what he might expect from a tribunal entirely under the influence of Bernard. On the other hand, he could at least hope that his friends in Rome would be able to upset Bernard's plans. We must therefore assume that Abelard fully realized the implications of what he was about to do when, on the following day at the appointed time, he entered the cathedral where the great assembly headed by the king and the bishops was awaiting him. After Bernard had read aloud a list of *capitula* for Abelard to admit as his and then either renounce or defend, or alternatively deny authorship of, he refused to make any form of statement on the grounds that he was appealing to Rome.[17]

Bernard and his party later stressed that Abelard had been subjected to no pressure. His freedom and safety had been guaranteed, and everyone had been prepared to listen to all he had to advance.[18] In a technical sense therefore it is certainly wrong for Berengar of Poitiers to assert that the synod condemned Abelard without being willing to hear him.[19] But one might well ask what value this freedom could have had for Abelard when he knew that the matter was already decided, and that he was to be condemned by his enemies. The various letters reflect the confusion Abelard's appeal evoked among those assembled. What was now to be done? It was impossible to ignore the appeal, although they were not convinced that it was in accordance with canon law.[20] Abelard had succeeded once more in upsetting Bernard's plans. Out of consideration for the pope, they decided to leave to him the decision as to Abelard's person, and to confine themselves to condemning nineteen propositions as heretical. In the reports to the pope, however, the action they wished him to take against Abelard was carefully set out.

After his appeal, Abelard left the church and the city. As he went from the church, his glance fell upon the well-known master, Gilbert de la Porrée. Upon seeing his colleague – an outstanding dialectician like himself and an admirer of the Greek philosophers – a quotation from Horace came to his mind: When your neighbour's wall is burning, it is your turn next![21] What appeared to be merely an elegant exit later proved a sombre prophecy. A few years later, Gilbert was accused of heresy by Bernard at the Synod of Rheims.[22] When Abelard had left, steps were taken to condemn the nineteen propositions put forward, and therewith the synod was concluded. All that remained was to inform the pope of the result of the proceedings. The reports were probably prepared before the bishops parted. Bernard considered it advisable to write on his own behalf, and episcopal letters were sent from Sens and Rheims. Both these are included in Bernard's collection of letters, and this is not without reason. The letter from Samson of Rheims in particular bears the unmistakable stamp of Bernard's style, using several of the phrases taken from his letters to the Roman prelates. Samson describes Abelard as a man from whom nothing is hidden, since he claims to understand everything through his intellect. A number of Bernard's terms of abuse find employment here once again. In addition, the current affair is brought into relation with the judgment at Soissons in 1121, precisely as Bernard had done in several of his Roman letters.[23] Though Bernard was probably also consulted when Henry of Sens drafted the letter from his Archdiocese – the official report of the proceedings – this relationship was not mentioned, as Geoffrey of Chartres, Abelard's friend at Soisson, was a co-signatory of the Sens letter.

In this second letter, emphasis was given to a point only hinted at by Samson: Abelard's dangerous influence upon student youth whom he had encouraged to discuss the Holy Trinity, resulting in the circulation of many unseemly things. In picturesque terms, Abelard is described as the centre of a pernicious furore, which right-minded men have attempted to halt in vain. At the same time, the bishops admit that they themselves had become very uneasy, but had done nothing about it. In a somewhat pathetic manner, the archbishop then tries to divorce himself from the invitation he had extended, on Abelard's initiative, to Bernard. Thereafter follows a description of what took place at Sens, and the letter ends with an earnest request to the pope to deprive Abelard of the opportunity to write and to teach.[24]

As well as writing to the pope, Bernard also sent letters to some of the cardinals in order to hasten the condemnation. Abelard's counter-stroke had of course deprived Bernard of an immediate victory. It is true that the synod had declared the nineteen *capitula* to be false and heretical, but unfortunately Abelard had not admitted to them. There is no doubt that Bernard was very concerned that Abelard, with his feared eloquence, might be able to turn the mood in Rome to his advantage, once he was given an opportunity to speak in his own cause. Nothing bears witness more clearly to Bernard's continuing sense of insecurity than this correspondence. There could be no question of allowing the matter to take its course quietly and peacefully; it was important to get a quick decision which would give Abelard no time for new counter-moves. The letter to the pope gives Bernard's version of what occurred before the meeting at Sens and on the day itself. This long letter is a brilliant example of Bernard's letter-writing art. Two features in particular have the touch of genius. First, the comparison between the earlier papal schism and Abelard's heresy; Bernard laments the misery of this life, which has now brought him face to face with the ambush of the dragon (Abelard) so soon after he had secured peace from the raging of the lion (a reference to the family name of the anti-pope, Anacletus II, Pier Leone). In this way he succeeds in reminding the pope of the services he had rendered in helping to overcome the schism. Secondly, the circumstance that Arnold of Brescia had joined Abelard is described as if Arnold and Abelard, 'the Italian bee and the French bee', had formed a league against the Church or, as Bernard plaintively expresses it, 'against the Lord and His anointed'. The two are compared with Goliath and his weapon-bearer, whose impudence increases in the belief that there is no David in the Israel camp. It is discreetly left to the pope himself to decide who is David, although Bernard ensures that this is not very difficult for him: 'When all have fled before him, he now challenges me to single combat!'

There is scarcely any doubt that these well-calculated reminders of two of the most disagreeable episodes in Innocent II's reign had their intended effect, although they had nothing at all to do with the matter at hand. The letter ends with a negative reference to Hyacinth: Bernard has no wish to describe the mischief Hyacinth did against him; he takes no heed of this, as Hyacinth spares not even the Roman Curia.[25] The same hint appears in the letter to Chancellor Haimeric, but he adds that Hyacinth also took the pope to task.[26] In this manner Bernard prepared the ground for the return home of the young sub-deacon, and neutralized the unpleasant testimony he was expected to give. The other letters to Rome of that period add nothing new. They warn of Abelard's arrival, briefly describe the content of his heresy and urge onwards the fight for the cause of Christ and for the threatened faith.[27]

While Bernard went about this work, Abelard was by no means idle. He went south, obviously with the intention of travelling to Rome; but he never reached there. He soon arrived at the famous monastery of Cluny, where he was kindly received by the abbot, Peter the Venerable. Here he began to write his defence. As there are no documents from the Synod of Sens, Abelard is the only contemporary source from which we can draw conclusions as to the nineteen *capitula* that were condemned; indeed, we know the number of the propositions only from him.[28] There now exist two different defence documents from the hand of Abelard; one is a brief *Confessio fidei*,[29] and the other an *Apologia* laid out on a grand scale, of which unfortunately we have only a fragment containing a refutation of the first proposition.[30] In both works Abelard sets out the propositions claimed to be heretical, but the two lists we can prepare on the basis of his accounts do not quite coincide. The *Confessio* very probably takes up a position on the *capitula* that Bernard had sent the pope together with his treatise, while the *Apologia* concerns the synod's *capitula*.[31] The *Confessio* should therefore be read as a personal defence against Bernard's treatise. This being the case, it probably came into being before the synod.[32] If this is not so, it must be assumed that he wrote it immediately after the departure from Sens, with the purpose of dissociating himself at once from the condemned heresies. Abelard's use of the list in Bernard's treatise could then be explained on the basis that he had not then learned of the exact wording of the synod's *capitula*. The purpose of the *Apologia* is completely clear. It is intended as a detailed refutation of the accusations with a view to the anticipated proceedings in Rome.

If one looks more closely at the *capitula*, it is possible to establish that some of them are in fact to be found in Abelard's writings: in the *Theologia*, the *Ethics* and the *Commentary on the Epistle to the Romans*. Others, however, it is impossible to trace; they undoubtedly originate from the work already referred to, *The Book of Sentences*, attributed to Abelard by Bernard but for which Abelard denied any responsibility. Many of them already appear in William of St Thierry's list, and most of them are to be found in Bernard's indictment. They centre around the doctrine of the Trinity, the atonement, the person of Christ, original sin and the concept of sin as a whole. We shall here refer to only the most significant: those *capitula* that have a direct connection with Abelard's writings.

The first proposition is not a quotation, but is claimed to

follow from Abelard's teaching on the Trinity. In translation it reads as follows: 'that the Father is the omnipotent power, the Son a certain power, and the Holy Ghost no power'. In their refutation of this, both William and Bernard maintain with great vehemence and intense wrath that the proposition follows from Abelard's explanation of the relationship between the divine Persons.[33] As already shown, Abelard uses the concepts of power, wisdom and goodness to characterize the three Persons. The conclusions of William and Bernard are to the following effect: the Son is wisdom, wisdom is a certain power (namely, to discern), consequently the Son is a certain power; the Holy Ghost is goodness, goodness is no power, consequently the Holy Ghost is no power. Abelard had already replied to this objection in the fifth edition of the *Theologia*. In the fragment of his *Apologia* that we have, he goes into more detail concerning this. As in the *Theologia*, linguistic logic is the means of establishing that the proposition rests upon a misunderstanding. Two words having the same meaning when taken in isolation can, when employed as predicates in a sentence, assume completely different meanings, so that one of the sentences must be affirmed and the other denied. For example, God (*Deus*) and divinity (*divinitas*) have precisely the same meaning, but whereas one might well say: 'God is man' or 'God has suffered', it would be false to say: 'Divinity is man' or 'Divinity has suffered'. In the same way, God and 'God's substance' are completely identical, but it is none the less false to say that 'God's substance' is born of the Virgin Mary. Several more examples are cited. Consequently, Abelard believes, it is no more than ignorance of dialectic that leads Bernard to draw the conclusion that the comparison of the Son with wisdom, and of the Holy Ghost with goodness, must mean that everything which can be said of wisdom (or goodness) can also be said of the Son (or the Holy Ghost). By the use of the concepts of power, wisdom and goodness, Abelard seeks to characterize the relationship between the Persons; it is on the basis of these propositions that Bernard draws his conclusions, as if it were a matter of comparing the share of the Son and the Holy Ghost in the divine attributes with that of the Father. We may certainly say that Bernard's misunderstanding is natural, but it is effectively rejected by

Abelard. The first and perhaps the most important proposition in the list of heresies consequently lacks any basis whatever in relation to Abelard's works. It is not only impossible anywhere to find the proposition itself, but neither had Abelard at any time believed what it implies.[34] After reading the small fragment of the *Apologia*, we understand more readily why Bernard was so anxious to avoid meeting Abelard on an equal footing, but we must also deeply regret that we are precluded from knowing how Abelard would have handled the remaining propositions.[35]

Abelard's draft of a doctrine of atonement in the *Commentary on the Epistle to the Romans* had greatly embittered Bernard; but when this is developed into a proposition to the effect that Christ did not become man to free us from the yoke of the devil it is no longer possible to recognize Abelard's original point, and it becomes comprehensible that in the *Confessio fidei* he finds no difficulty in affirming the opposite. It is true to say that Abelard had sought to put an end to the discussion about the devil's right, and it is clear enough that his doctrine of the atonement took a new line; he can be distinguished from his contemporaries by his wish to see no juridical compulsion in the form of a payment for sin. But it cannot be said that the condemned proposition can with justice be fastened upon him.[36]

There was rather more success with a number of propositions concerned with Abelard's concept of sin. The condemnation of a proposition to the effect that we, from Adam onwards, have brought not guilt upon ourselves but only punishment can therefore be understood. William had already attacked Abelard on this point, probably on the basis of the *Book of Sentences*.[37] In the *Commentary on the Epistle to the Romans*, Abelard took the opportunity to advance his views on original sin. He says here, precisely as in the *Ethica*, that sin in the true sense means the soul's guilt and contempt of God, but that the expression is also used for the punishment that follows the sin or which we are considered to have become liable to because of the sin.[38] Consequently, Abelard must maintain that original sin is more a matter of punishment than of sin in the true sense, since small children cannot despise God. That we have sinned in Adam then signifies that we are condemned eternally because of his sin, if the remedies of the divine Sacraments do not come to our aid.[39] The basic viewpoint is not very different from that found in Anselm of Canterbury, who also saw original sin primarily as a liability imposed upon us.[40] But Abelard felt it advisable even so to make a few reservations at the end. He therefore concludes his theory of original sin with the comment that what he has said should be taken more as an expression of opinion than as a firm conviction.[41] But this, as we shall see, was not sufficient to save him from becoming the object of suspicion.

There is no difficulty in appreciating that the basic moral viewpoint — that is, the whole ethic of intention — must have caused offence. William was also the pioneer here.[42] The concept that those who crucified Christ did not sin because they acted in ignorance is condemned, as also are the demarcations Abelard employs in order to reach a conclusion as to what is the true good (or evil) in an action.[43] But as these propositions, in common with the other *capitula*, have been torn away from their context, it is difficult to decide in what light they were regarded by the synod, and whether the synod's understanding of them bore any relation to Abelard's intention. At all events, they were condemned without the alleged author being heard.

In the *Confessio fidei*, Abelard provides a brief summary of the *capitula*, and also expresses his opinion on Bernard's attack. 'It is a well-known saying: Nothing is so well said that it cannot be distorted.' With these words he introduces, and thereby immediately professes, his defence. He repudiates all the *capitula*, either by a denial of ever having written in this way or by giving an explanation attributing to the proposition a meaning different from Bernard's. As concerns Bernard's motives, Abelard has no doubt: he acted either from malice or from ignorance. Abelard concedes that he — who has spoken so much in the schools — may have failed, but he calls upon God to witness that it was never from malice or pride. He has, he says, always been and always will be prepared to correct himself. With a direct reference to one of Bernard's phrases, he contests ever having taught anything in secret.[44] His books have always been publicly available. He denies having written the *Book of Sentences* referred to by Bernard, and in Bernard's use of it he can see only the usual malice or ignorance. Finally, Abelard reminds his 'friend' that love enjoins one not to bring shame upon one's neighbour, and when in doubt to interpret everything in the best sense. This conclusion perhaps suggests that the paper was written *before* the synod as a last invitation to Bernard to withdraw.

The *Apologia*, which we must assume was begun by Abelard immediately after his arrival at Cluny, is also directed against Bernard, who is shown no mercy. Abelard has long tolerated his slander in the expectation that he would desist, either from fear of sin or out of respect for normal behaviour. But as it is now obvious that Bernard continues as he began, Abelard is forced to deal with him. Bernard is not content, like the Devil interpreting the Bible, to construe wrongly while using the correct words, but alters both sense and words. As we have said, Abelard's basic standpoint in refuting the first proposition is that Bernard has misunderstood him completely for the simple reason that he is unversed in dialectic, and consequently has no idea how such a problem should be examined.

Abelard was not subdued by the events at Sens. Ready to fight as always, he prepared himself for the next phase. That part of the *Apologia* we have shows very clearly that Abelard's anger was as unrelenting as Bernard's. The prospect of a hearing in Rome appears not to have worried him; at least it did nothing to weaken his fighting spirit. But he was proved wrong in his belief that he would be given an opportunity to fight for his cause at the Curia. This time it was Bernard who had the last word.

CHAPTER 9
Epilogue

While Abelard was waiting at Cluny with sharpened pen, preparing what he certainly hoped would be the literary destruction of Bernard, his opponent's express messenger was hastening towards Rome with the letters, which this time had the intended effect. As early as July 16th, not quite a month and a half after the synod, Pope Innocent II despatched two letters: to the Archbishops of Rheims and Sens and to the Abbot of Clairvaux. In one of these he confirmed the verdict of the synod on the nineteen *capitula* and himself condemned Abelard as a heretic, forbidding him to continue writing; all his followers, including expressly Arnold of Brescia, were excommunicated. In the other letter, the pope gave orders for Abelard to be placed in the custody of a monastery and for his books to be burnt wherever they were to be found. It was left to Bernard and the archbishops to decide upon Abelard's place of confinement.[1] Geoffrey of Auxerre writes that the pope himself set up a stake in St Peter's for the burning of the books.[2] However, not all Abelard's books within the area of Rome were burnt, for Pope Celestine II was able a few years later to present his native town with copies of them! He knew what he was about, since he was none other than Abelard's old benefactor, Guy of Castello.[3]

If we bear in mind the great distance between Sens and Rome and the postal services of the period, it becomes apparent that there had been no delay in Rome. There had been very little time to deal with the matter, but apart from this aspect Abelard was convicted without being heard. Although the nineteen propositions were considered to be heretical, and therefore had to be condemned, it still remained to be proved, before Abelard himself was condemned, that he acknowledged them as his. The bishops excused their judgment on the propositions by saying that Abelard himself had chosen his judges – indeed had fixed the time and place – and it was therefore his own fault if he would not speak, although given an opportunity to do so.[4] This statement can perhaps be contested, since it was scarcely an inquisitorial hearing that Abelard had agreed with the archbishop. The bishops however avoided passing judgment on Abelard's person, realizing that, as he had said nothing, it would be incorrect to do so. The pope however allowed no such considerations to obstruct him. It must be assumed that Bernard's personal prestige had decided the issue. In that sense Bernard can be awarded all the honours for having secured Abelard's condemnation, the pope in his letter permitting him to share these honours with the bishops.

Without doubt, this condemnation came as a great surprise to Abelard. The procedure was so irregular that the possibility would never have occurred to him. The information probably reached him while he was still preparing his defence. We do not know whether he broke off his work on the *Apologia* after this; the existing fragment has been interrupted in the middle of a sentence, but there is hope that one day the continuation will be found, however long this may be. Abelard and Bernard shared the current concept of heresy: it was not so much the wrong opinion itself as the obstinate persistence in it that was heretical. Bernard believed this to be precisely what he saw in Abelard, and he therefore did not rest until he had forced Abelard to be silent. The events following the condemnation proved him wrong.

Abelard submitted without argument as a dutiful son of the Church. In this difficult situation he did not forget Heloïse. It is in a letter to her that he writes the often-quoted words: 'I do not wish to be a philosopher by dissociating myself from Paul; I do not wish to be an Aristotle by separating myself from Christ, since there is no other name under heaven by which I can be saved.' He assures her that he has established his conscience upon the rock on which Christ has built His Church. Then follows a statement of faith in the Holy Trinity with special emphasis on the points found wanting in his books: the absolute equality of the Persons and a clear rejection of Arius and Sabellius. We do not know when this letter was written – probably immediately after the condemnation at Sens; he wished to reassure Heloïse immediately, as he knew she would be unhappy about the events at the synod. Perhaps we may be permitted to surmise that, at the time his enemies were assailing him, he desired for his own comfort to turn once more to her whose love would have appeared to him as the fortress of his being.

The venerable Abbot Peter of Cluny was not content only to express his sympathy for Abelard, and immediately after the papal judgment he took the initiative towards a reconciliation. With the co-operation of the Abbot of Cîteaux, he succeeded in arranging a meeting between Abelard and Bernard. Abelard travelled to Clairvaux, where he had a peaceable reunion with Bernard. We are unaware of the details of these discussions, as they are suppressed by Bernard's biographers. Bernard's pleasure would have been somewhat mixed. He could scarcely refuse to welcome Abelard's willingness to co-operate, but this very fact would have made him doubt the justification for his own actions. The man he had succeeded in having condemned as a heretic had now shown that he completely lacked the obstinacy of a heretic. Bernard's doctrinal victory was consequently turned into a moral defeat.

Peter the Venerable informed the pope of these matters, and at the same time asked permission to keep Abelard in his monastery for the rest of his days. This coincided with Abelard's own wishes, and so it was arranged. The pope gave his permission and lifted Abelard's sentence without objection.[5]

In his letter to the pope, Peter the Venerable hints that Abelard's days would not be many. His health was somewhat poor, and just over a year and a half after his arrival at Cluny, in April 1142, he died. At that time he had been moved to a daughter house of Cluny which was thought to have a healthier climate. Although the last period of his life was marked by great physical adversity, there is nothing to suggest that the condemnation had broken him; he worked on tirelessly to the last.

He had, it is true, submitted to the judgment of the Church, but this in no way meant that, from fear or from any sudden distrust in his powers of judgment, he spurned his own achievements. In his last unfinished work, *The Dialogue between a Jew, a Philosopher and a Christian*, he continues along his usual path and proudly refers to the *Theologia* as an admirable piece of work. Abelard here awards himself the very same worth as that found in his autobiography; he is the greatest master of his time whose legitimate reputation neither envy nor persecution has been able to assail.[6]

Against this background, it is strange to read Peter the Venerable's account of Abelard's life at Cluny, given in a letter to Heloïse after Abelard's death. 'However great or however beautiful the testimony that Cluny can pay to his holy, humble and pious life among us, this cannot be expressed in a few words. For, if I am not mistaken, I remember having seen no person to compare with him in humility, both as to habit and behaviour.... And although, because I wished it, he occupied a high rank among the great host of our brothers, one would be forced, upon seeing his miserable clothing, to believe him the most inferior of all.' The abbot continues by telling how Abelard was content with the least possible in all things; he spent his time reading and praying, and only spoke when he was asked to preach to the brothers or to instruct them in their reading.[7]

It accords well with this way of life that Abelard immediately submitted to the pope's verdict and became reconciled with Bernard. It proves to us that the instructions Abelard had given Heloïse and her nuns in sermons and letters were no empty words, but were deeply rooted in his own experience. Perhaps the conversation with Bernard also touched upon the ascetic life they had in common. Here at least was an area where they could meet. In the field of objective theology, however, Abelard acknowledged no submission; he was convinced of the rectitude of his actions. He submitted to the decision of the Church because he was not and never had been the freebooter Bernard thought him to be, and he submitted with a good conscience because he believed his theology to be in conformity with Church doctrine. Submission was to him a testimony that accorded with his theology, and for that very reason it signified no change of mind on his part. Even after his readmission to the Church and his reconciliation with Bernard, he continued to look upon the attack as an expression of envy or ignorance. The contrast between personal humility and high arrogance as soon as his theological work was questioned is therefore only apparent. He himself was in no difficulty on this point.

It appears that Abelard's move to the monastery of St Marcel in the neighbourhood of Chalon had in fact a favourable effect upon his health. Peter the Venerable writes concerning this: 'Here he resumed his old studies, so far as his weakness permitted, and he was always engrossed in his books. Similarly, as we read of Gregory the Great, he allowed no moment to pass unused, but was always praying, reading, writing or dictating.' Illness interrupted him in the middle of his work, and because of his low resistance it quickly gained the upper hand. Peter ends his account of Abelard's last hours by addressing himself directly to Heloïse, whom he tries to console by saying that Christ will preserve him for her until the time when God, in the Second Coming of the Lord, will return him to her.[8] This letter was in reply to Heloïse, who had written to Cluny, probably immediately after hearing the rumour of Abelard's death, requesting that Abelard's body be transferred to the Paraclete.[9] This in fact occurred. In a letter to Peter the Venerable, Heloïse thanks him for a visit to the Paraclete and asks him to send her a letter embodying an absolution for Abelard, which she can hang on his grave. At the same time, she asks the abbot to secure for their son, Astrolabius, a prebend either at Notre Dame in Paris or at another cathedral.[10] With the reply came the desired absolution for Abelard; this apart, Peter promised to do what he could for Astrolabius.[11]

Abelard's death did not, as Heloïse had once said it would in a letter to him,[12] end her own life. It was more than twenty years later that the first abbess of the Paraclete died and was laid in the grave where her beloved rested.

Although the Abelard affair had been concluded with the pope's sentence and Abelard's submission, and although Bernard had consequently won a complete victory, there was still one person who dared to speak against this powerful man. Berengar of Poitiers, a disciple of Abelard, wrote a defence of his teacher

that, in style and content, has more the nature of an attack on
Bernard. This little monograph contributes objectively only very
little to the dispute, but it probably reflects quite well the mood
in Abelard's camp. The treatise begins with a somewhat
equivocal reference to Bernard's reputation for eloquence and
holiness. Berengar then describes the encounter at Sens and
reproaches Bernard for his harshness. By way of testimony to
Abelard's orthodoxy he quotes the extract already referred to
from the letter to Heloïse. Finally, he enters into a direct attack
upon Bernard's own theology, and scoffs at his sermons on the
Song of Songs. Several of Bernard's statements are branded as
heretical, with a view to showing what little right Bernard had
to direct an accusation of heresy against others. Berengar seems
to have been a somewhat arrogant young man, who delighted
in his well-phrased insults and apt quotations from the classics.
Even so, it would be wrong to reject him out of hand. Here and
there his accusations hit the mark, for example when he writes
as follows about Bernard's sermon at Sens: 'You said in your
address to the people that they should offer prayers to God for
him [that is, for Abelard]; but inwardly you prepared to eject
him from Christendom.'[13] If we ignore the sarcasm, much of
which is of studied virulence, there still remains one point that
appears to stem from a sincere love of Abelard: Berengar does
not deny that Abelard may have erred, but he reproaches
Bernard for showing no mercy. 'But, say the supporters of the
abbot, he sought to lead Peter to the right road. If, my good
man, it was your intention to lead Peter back to the purity of
the Faith, why then did you wish, in the sight of the people, to
brand him with the mark of eternal damnation? And, on the
other hand, in depriving Peter of the love of the people, how
then did you intend to guide him? By comparing these facts,
one comes to the conclusion that it was not eagerness to guide
but the desire for personal revenge that awoke your burning
wrath against Peter. Gloriously has the prophet said: The
righteous guide me in mercy. For where mercy is lacking there
can be no talk of reproof by the righteous but only of the crude
barbarism of a tyrant.'[14] Berengar concedes that several of the
Sens propositions were said and written by Abelard, but in some
of them he had no part. He promises to go into this in more detail

in a later treatise, but for the moment his purpose was to reject Bernard's right to brand Abelard with the name of heretic.[15]

The new treatise, in which Berengar was to discuss in more detail the accusations against Abelard, he unfortunately never succeeded in writing. Had he done so, this might well have helped us to determine more precisely the origin of those propositions not to be found in Abelard's works. Berengar soon had other things to think about; his attack on Bernard gave rise to much indignation, and he was forced to flee. From his exile he wrote seeking reconciliation with the many he had offended, including the anchorites at La Grande Chartreuse. Among other points, he mentions one objection put forward against his treatise which, whether consciously or not, has often lain behind evaluations of the dispute between Bernard and Abelard: How dare you speak against the saintly man! As for the rest, he excuses himself by his youth, and states that he has not published his promised continuation because he has no wish to protect the rejected *capitula*. He cannot call back the first treatise, since it has been spread throughout France and Italy in a great number of copies, but he is prepared to show his penitence by declaring that all he has said against the man of God, Bernard, should be read as a jest, and not taken seriously.[16] It appears reasonable to conclude from the letter that Berengar had created quite a sensation, but that he had been forced to see that it was beyond his powers to continue the struggle.[17]

Whereas Berengar of Poitiers was made to pay heavily for his audacity towards Bernard, the powerful Abbot of Cluny could permit himself to express his opinion freely. This he did in an epitaph on Abelard which gives the impression almost of a polemic against Bernard. There cannot be the slightest doubt that Peter the Venerable's disapproval of Bernard's behaviour was extreme. Although the leader of the Cluniacs was one of those placid people who find greater satisfaction in negotiating peace than in hunting down opponents, he had by no means shared the general admiration of Bernard. Apart from Peter the Venerable, there were few who dared to speak for Abelard. It is clear that, against the background of the events following the Synod of Sens, Abelard's supporters at the Curia in Rome felt themselves not strong enough openly to champion his cause.

Arnold of Brescia appeared as a master in Paris for a short time, but although he may well have defended Abelard, his real concern – the struggle against the landed property of the Church – was of quite a different nature. In any event, this restless man soon set out on his wanderings again, pursued far beyond the frontiers of France by the saintly Bernard. A far more important development was that Abelard's successor at Mont Ste Geneviève, the British-born Robert of Melun, openly defended his teaching on the Holy Trinity and used his terminology.[18] Further proof that Abelard's use of the three concepts of power, wisdom and goodness in relation to the three divine persons by no means gave rise to universal suspicion may be found in Richard of St Victor's monograph *On the Holy Trinity*. The school of the Victorines was close to Bernard, but in spite of this the dispute over Abelard's theology appears to have made no impression on Richard. These examples of a positive attitude are however rather isolated in the face of the general silence on Abelard in later scholastic theology. He fades out of discussion in a singular manner.

There can be no doubt of the reason for this: Bernard's influence was strong enough to erase Abelard's name. The Saint's opinions came to determine the contemporary assessment, as well as that of later times. So it came about that the schoolmen of the thirteenth century were directly concerned with Abelard only to a limited extent. Bernard's accusations simply lived on. They determined the historical image of Abelard's theology that remained relatively undisputed until there commenced, during the latter part of the nineteenth century, the recrudescence of interest in the thought of the Middle Ages.[19] Dante for example does not mention Abelard in *The Divine Comedy*, and a writer such as Pope could say in the eighteenth century that Abelard was known mainly for his love affair with Heloïse. It might therefore appear that Bernard had won hands down. But it was not quite so clear-cut.

In his epitaph on Abelard, Peter the Venerable refers to him as 'the Socrates of the Gauls, the great Plato of the West, our Aristotle'. He acclaims him as a logician equal to or better than all before him, able to dominate all things by the power of reason and the art of discourse. But, he adds, he won his greatest victory when he came to Cluny and truly entered into Christ's philosophy.[20] This picture of Abelard as the great thinker and intellectual who won respect as a follower of Christ in the asceticism of the monastery is painted with no reference whatever to the condemnation at Sens and its confirmation by the pope; Peter could permit himself to act in this way since he had no need to fear Bernard's wrath. But it is curious that this picture appears to correspond precisely to the general impression one has formed of Abelard. Outside the close circle of theologians and Bernard's followers, Abelard was remembered after his death as the acute thinker and the meritorious monk. Several of the monastic chroniclers who make a reference to him on the occasion of his death refer in particular to the foundation of the Paraclete.[21] In many cases there is not one word about the condemnation for heresy.

This goes some way to show the limited significance inquisitorial proceedings still had upon the reputation of the accused at that time. In this connection, we may call to mind what little effect the drastic sentence at Soissons in 1121 had had upon Abelard's career. Another example of this is the case of Gilbert de la Porrée, who was accused of heresy in 1148 at a synod in Rheims. It is true that some of his opinions were denounced as heretical, but Gilbert himself remained unchallenged and returned home to his episcopal seat at Poitiers, where he remained until his death without his prestige having suffered the least damage. We must consequently be on guard against over-estimating the interest in, or the importance of, theological disputes. The Church in general, and this means first and foremost the ordinary clergy and the monasteries, were only very little affected by these matters; they were impressed by Abelard's acuteness and knowledge, but this apart his contributions as a monk and as the founder of a monastery were better understood.

Such recognition was not however sufficient to keep his name alive in the memory of later times; there were many monks and founders of monasteries, and not a few with a far greater reputation than Abelard. A renown such as his would necessarily be of a fairly local nature, and only to a limited extent could it survive those who had seen or heard him in the flesh. It was as a thinker that Abelard himself wished to be known, and it was indeed as a thinker that he is recognized by posterity, although until the end of the nineteenth century there was ignorance of this aspect of him. In the light of the many contemporary witnesses to his unrivalled prestige, it is easy enough to conjecture that the effects of his extensive influence could not have been erased simply by a papal letter. But it was not until H. Denifle found a number of manuscripts incontestably written by disciples of Abelard that one could speak with certainty of the existence of a school of Abelard. Since then research has continued, and new finds have come to light. It can consequently be established that by about the middle of the twelfth century theology was the subject of lectures at many important seats of learning, Abelard's *Theologia* being the undisputed source of inspiration. On the basis of the manuscripts we now have, this influence can be traced far beyond the borders of France; disciples of Abelard have come to light in Italy, Austria and England. The important centre of study at Bologna counted several of them, including the famous Roland Bandinelli who later became Pope Alexander III.[22] Among Abelard's friends at the Curia, apart from Guy of Castello (Celestine II), his comrade-in-arms at Sens, Hyacinth, also came to occupy the papal chair under the title of Celestine III. The fact that three popes and a multitude of cardinals, archbishops and bishops were among Abelard's adherents should not be taken to suggest that any kind of coherent 'Abelard party' occupied an especially prominent position in the period following 1142, but on the other hand it is a further proof of the great attraction his teaching exercised.

The 'monastic' party continued the struggle against this new theology. On several occasions Abelard is conjured up to frighten and to warn. Consequently, when later the zealous William of St Thierry attacked William of Conches (one of the school of Chartres' famous philosophers), he immediately submitted to the attack, very probably because the accusation that he had been concerned in Abelard's heresies showed him where the matter would lead.[23] In Germany, Gerhoch of Reichersberg was an energetic opponent of the new theology, and his antagonists included Abelard's pupils. The Victorines also produced a castigator of the former master in Walter of St Victor, who in a paper bearing the title *Against the four labyrinths of France*, dating from about 1175, described the theology of the new masters, including, besides Abelard, Peter the Lombard, as endangering the Church.[24]

Peter the Lombard, who ended his career as Bishop of Paris, was also at one time Abelard's pupil before he himself became a master. His most important work, *The Books of the Sentences*, gained enormous popularity and soon became the acknowledged theological text book at the universities. Consequently, until the end of the Middle Ages, this was the text upon which every theologian with academic ambitions had to comment at one time or another during his career. In our context, it is therefore significant that Peter the Lombard – without naming Abelard – leans heavily on his books.[25] But Peter is also identified with Abelard's efforts in another way. First, he uses the method set out by Abelard in *Sic et non*, and there is no doubt that this work was a mine of information for him and many others when it became necessary to find quotations from the Fathers to illustrate the various problems. But an influence of a negative kind can also be suggested: in his Prologue, Peter the Lombard sharply dissociates himself from all philosophy, proclaiming that he will confine himself to the Bible and the holy Fathers. We may see in this a further proof of the fear of philosophical studies aroused among masters of the period by the dispute between Abelard and Bernard; indeed, Bernard had succeeded in delaying the penetration of philosophy into theology. In addition to the Lombard's Sentences, another work should also be mentioned which has a connection with Abelard: the *Summa Sententiarum*. This monograph was previously thought to be the work of Hugh of St Victor, but this is probably incorrect. There is no agreement as to whom we should consider to be the author, but in any event it originated in Parisian surroundings at about the middle of the century. Here also the arrangement of the material and many of the views expressed are influenced by Abelard. The manuscripts discovered show that this monograph had an immense dissemination, ironically enough even in the Cistercian monasteries.[26]

Although only few dared to mention his name, Abelard lived on. More recent research shows clearly that, in the Abelard affair, Bernard suffered a thorough defeat. He was able to destroy

Abelard himself, but to stop the movement Abelard had started was beyond the power of Bernard or of any pope. In spite of all, it was to be Abelard and not his opponents who influenced the development of academic teaching in the period following. He was the first to sketch out a plan for a really comprehensive, independent discussion of all religious dogma. In his dialectic he had indicated a method for such a perceptive interpretation of the material handed down by his forerunners. He had also made tradition itself more comprehensible in his formidable collection of relevant material (*Sic et non*). In his treatment of ethical problems, he had set new tasks for his successors. In all this, he was motivated by a passionate desire to understand, which was inspired by his research into the classical tradition. His activities became a danger to the traditionalism that dominated the reform movement led by Bernard, because he would not desist when he came face to face with Christian tradition. Viewed in this perspective, his contest with Bernard illustrates one of the frequent clashes in the history of the Church, when traditionalism attempts to prevent the injection of life into tradition by a perceptive apprehension of it. The new academic trend – the twelfth century Renaissance – posed to the traditional interpretation of life a number of questions that demanded answers. Those who, under the effect of the humanism that accompanied the recrudescence of classical studies, looked upon the questions as impertinent had, in spite of resistance, to give them their attention. It is strange that these were the very people to herald the period in European thought referred to as the age of the schoolmen.

Abelard is only one among many, but because of his unique influence he is one of those who contributed most to the change in the intellectual climate that led to the birth of the universities. As this movement, which he among others had set in motion, took a firmer form, some of the agitation and confusion that characterized the twelfth century disappeared. Access to the ethics and metaphysics of Aristotle created new problems, and in doing so changed the manner of approach to the problems. Impressive philosophical systems of an extent and vision far beyond what was known at the time of Abelard were created. The method that Abelard – more than any other – established was further elaborated, and was employed in theological speculations of vast dimensions; but it cannot be denied that much was lost in the process. It was Abelard's difficult task to interpret Christian belief from the basis of the classical-humanist tradition. This tradition he had constantly to keep before him, for as a member of mankind he could not avoid acknowledging the heritage of the ancient world. But this interpretative task was to be replaced by the creation of an all-embracing synthesis in which the classical tradition – by now almost exclusively represented by Aristotle – was rendered harmless by becoming reduced to no more than the lowest stratum in a system of thought crowned by divine authority. Occupied with the erection of this system – and in time also with pulling it down again – Abelard's successors completely forgot that his concept had been that the relationship between the Christian faith and classical tradition poses a problem that can only be determined *historically*, in the sense that the solution can never be passed on but must be sought anew by each generation. But it was also forgotten that the problem was one of interpreting Revelation in the light of man's constantly changing circumstances; instead, the schoolmen sought to create a rational system of a timeless character – and they themselves brought about its collapse even before the intervention of external criticism in the form of humanism and reformation.

In another historical perspective, however, it was decisive that the work started by Abelard and those similarly disposed continued as an unceasing movement. Authority had been made the subject of question, and the questioning could not again be silenced. Although much of what occupied the thinkers of the Middle Ages seems strange to us, it would be foolish to feel – certainly to express – any superiority in relation to these men. They were trying to unravel the same human condition that concerns us, and in their endeavours they were neither better nor worse than we are. No 'development', no 'advance', is of any help here. The conflict between Bernard and Abelard was an expression of two completely different concepts of life; most of us alive today would probably find it difficult to identify ourselves with either of them. We think in a different way, we understand existence in a manner different from them; but even so, to be different is not to be either better or more correct.

GENERAL BIBLIOGRAPHY

It is not the intention to set out here a comprehensive or fully representative bibliography, as this does not correspond to the nature of this study, but to indicate, in general, easily accessible literature for a further study of the subject. Particular points raised in the text are discussed in the notes to each chapter which follow the bibliography.

Editions marked with an asterisk * are in paperback.

The abbreviation of the titles of books referred to in the notes is indicated by the use of square brackets [ ], enclosing that part of the reference which will be omitted.

GENERAL WORKS

F. Coppleston, *History of Philosophy* (London 1952).

A. Fliche and V. Martin, *Histoire de l'église*, VIII, IX, XIII (Paris 1946, 1948, 1951).

J. de Ghellinck, *La littérature latine au moyen âge* (Paris 1939).

[E.] Gilson, [*History of Christian Philosophy in the Middle Ages*] (London 1955).

——, *L'esprit de la philosophie médiévale* (2. ed. Paris 1944; Eng. trans. New York 1948).

[M.] Grabmann, [*Die Geschichte der Scholastische Methode*] (Freiburg-im-Breisgau 1909, 1911).

C. H. Haskins, *The Rise of Universities* (New York 1923, repr. 1957*).

M. D. Knowles, *The Evolution of Medieval Thought* (London 1962).

J. Leclercq, *L'amour des lettres et le désir de dieu* (Paris 1957).

M. Manitius, *Geschichte der Lateinischen Literatur des Mittelalters* (Leipzig 1911–1931).

H. Rashdall, *The Universities of Europe in the Middle Ages*, ed. F. M. Powicke and A. B. Emden (Oxford 1936).

[R.] Seeberg [*Lehrbuch der Dogmengeschichte*, III] (3. ed. Leipzig 1913).

B. Smalley, *The Study of the Bible in the Middle Ages* (2. ed. Oxford 1952).

R. W. Southern, *The Making of the Middle Ages* (London 1953, repr. 1967*).

[F.] Ueberweg- [B. Geyer, *Grundriss der Geschichte der Philosophie, Die Patristische und Scholastische Philosophie*] (11. ed. Berlin 1928, repr. Basel 1951).

M. de Wulf, *Histoire de la philosophie médiévale* (6. ed. Louvain 1934–1947, Eng. trans. London 1935–47).

Dictionnaire de théologie catholique.

Dictionnaire d'histoire et de géographie ecclesiastique.

THE TWELFTH-CENTURY RENAISSANCE

[M-D.] Chenu, [*La théologie au douzieme siècle*] (Paris 1957).

[J-F.] Genest, [*Les moralistes antiques chez les humanistes et les mystiques du xiie siècle*] (Poitiers 1957, typescript).

[J. de] Ghellinck, *L'essor de la littérature latine au xiie siècle* (Brussels and Paris 1946).

—— [*Le mouvement théologique du xiie siècle*] (2 ed. Bruges 1948).

[C. H.] Haskins, [*The Renaissance of the Twelfth Century*] (Cambridge, Mass., 1927, repr. New York 1957*).

——, *Studies in the History of Medieval Science* (Cambridge, Mass., 1924).

A. M. Landgraf, *Einführung in die Geschichte der Theologischen Literatur der Frühscholastik* (Ratisbon 1948).

——, *Dogmengeschichte der Frühscholastik*, I–IV (Ratisbon 1952ff.).

[L.] Ott, ['Untersuchungen zur Theologischen Briefliteratur der Frühscholastik'], Beiträge [*zur Geschichte der Philosophie und Theologie des Mittelalters*], XXXIV (Münster 1937).

[G.] Paré, [A. Brunet and P. Tremblay, *La renaissance du xiie siècle. Les ecoles et l'enseignement*] (Paris 1933).

[R. L.] Poole, [*Illustrations of the History of Medieval Thought and Learning*] (2. ed. Oxford 1920, repr. 1960).

F. van Steenberghen, *Aristotle in the West* (Louvain 1955).

ST ANSELM OF CANTERBURY

[S.] *Anselmi Opera* [*Omnia*], I–VI, ed. F. S. Schmitt (Rome and Edinburgh 1958–61).

Eadmer, *The Life of St Anselm*, ed. R. W. Southern (Edinburgh 1962.

——, *Historum novorum in anglia*, trans. G. Bosanquet (London 1964).

R. W. Southern, *St Anselm and his Biographer* (Cambridge 1963).

R. W. Church, *St Anselm* (London 1870).

A. Wilmart, *Auteurs spirituels et textes dévots du moyen age latin* (Paris 1932).

ST BERNARD

[S.] Bernardi, *Opera*, [ed. J. P.] Migne, [*Patrologiae cursus completus series latina*], CLXXXII-CLXXXV (Paris 1879).

A new edition of St Bernard's works is in course of preparation. To date four volumes have appeared:

Sancti Bernardi opera I, 'Sermones super Cantica Canticorum', 1–35, ed. J. Leclercq, C. H. Talbot, H. M. Rochais (Rome 1957), II, 'Sermones super Cantica Canticorum', 36–86, ed. J. Leclercq, C. H. Talbot, H. M. Rochais and C. Mohrmann (Rome 1958), III, 'Tractatus et opuscula', ed. J. Leclercq and H. M. Rochais (Rome 1963), IV, 'Sermones' I, ed. J. Leclercq and H. M. Rochais (Rome 1966).

St Bernard's letters have been translated by B. S. James, *The Letters of Saint Bernard of Clairvaux* (London 1953).

The standard biographies are still:

[E.] Vacandard, [*Vie de St Bernard*] (Paris 1894, repr. 1920).
W. Williams, *Saint Bernard of Clairvaux* (Manchester 1935, repr. 1952).

See also:

[E.] Gilson, [*The*] *Mystical Theology* [*of Saint Bernard*] (London 1944, repr. 1955. This work has been used as the basis for the discussion of Bernard's theology in Chapter VI.
[R.] Klibansky, ['Peter Abailard and Bernard of Clairvaux', 'A Letter by Abailard'], *Medieval and Renaissance Studies* V (London 1961).

The occasion, in 1953, of the eighth centenary of Bernard's death saw the production of a number of important collections dealing with the saint's life and writings:

[*Bernhard von Clairvaux*], *Mönch and Mystiker*, [Internationaler Bernhard-kongress, Mainz 1953] (Wiesbaden 1955).
[J.] Leclercq, 'Etudes [sur Saint Bernard et le texte de ses ecrits'], *Analecta Sacri Ordinis Cisterciensis*, IX, 1–2 (Rome 1953).
'Saint Bernard Théologien', *Analecta sacri ordinis cisterciensis*, IX, 3–4 (Rome 1953).
Bernard de Clairvaux, 'Commission d'histoire de L'ordre de cîteaux III' (Dijon 1953).
'Mélanges Saint Bernard', *xxive Congrès de L'association bourguignonne des sociétés savantes* (Dijon 1953).

In these collections see particularly:

[J.] Leclercq, ['S. Bernard et la] théologie monastique [du xiie siècle'], in *Saint Bernard théologien*, pp. 7–28.
[E.] Kleineidam, ['Wissen, Wissenschaft, Theologie bei Bernhard von Clairvaux, I'] in *Mönch und Mystiker*.

ABELARD

[*Petri*] *Abaelardi Opera*, [ed. V. Cousin], 2 vols (Paris 1849, 1859).

[*Ouvrages inédites d'Abelard*, ed. V.] Cousin (Paris 1836).

Petri Abelardi Opera, Migne CLXXVIII (Paris 1855).

[B.] Geyer, ['Peter Abaelards Philosophische Schriften'], *Beiträge* XXI, i–iv (Münster 1919–33).

[H.] Ostlender, ['P. Abälards] Theologia Summi Boni', [*Beiträge etc*] XXXV, ii–iii (Münster 1936).

——, ['Die] Theologia Scholarium [des P. Abälards', in *Aus der Geisteswelt des Mittelalters*], *Beiträge* Suppl. III (Münster 1935).

[L. M. de] Rjik, [*Dialectica*], *Wijsgerige Teksten en Stud* (Assen 1956).

[P.] Ruf [and M.] Grabmann, ['Ein Neuaufgefundenes Bruchstück der Apologia Abaelards']. *Sitzungsberichte der Bayerischen Akademie der Wissenschaften, Philologisch-historische Abt.*, Heft V (Munich 1930).

F. P. G. Guizot, *Abailard et Héloïse, Essai historique, suivie des Lettres d'Abailard et d'Héloïse* (Paris 1856).

M. de Gandillac, *Oeuvres choisies d'Abelard* (Paris 1945).

E. Gilson and J. T. Muckle, Abelard's Letter of Consolation to a Friend 'Historia Calamitatum', *Medieval Studies* XII (Toronto 1950).

[J. Monfrin], H[*istoria*] C[*alamitatum*] (Paris 1959).

J. T. Muckle, *The Story of Abelard's Adversities* (Toronto 1954).

——, 'The Personal Letters of Abelard and Heloïse', *Medieval Studies* XV (Toronto 1953).

William of St Thierry, [*Opera*], Migne CLXXX (Paris 1855).

Otto of Freising, [*The Deeds of Frederick Barbarossa*], trans. C. C. Mierow and R. Emery (New York 1953).

[John of Salisbury], *Metalogicon*, [trans. D. D. McGarry] (Berkeley and Los Angeles 1955).

——, *The Historia Pontificalis*, trans. M. Chibnall (Edinburgh 1956).

'Chronicum Mauriniacense', ed. G. Waitz, *Monumenta Germaniae Historica, Scriptores Rerum Germanicarum*, XXVI (Hanover 1882), pp. 37–45.

J. R. McCallum, *Abelard's Christian Theology* (Oxford 1948).

[J.] Cottiaux ['La conception de la théologie chez Abelard'], *Revue d'histoire ecclesiastique*, XXVIII (Louvain 1932), pp. 247–95, 533–51, 788–828.

[H.] Ostlender, ['Die] Sentenzenbücher [der Schule Abaelards'], *Theologische Quartalschrift*, CXVII (Tübingen 1936).

[N. A.] Sidorova, ['Abelard et son époque'], *Cahiers d'histoire mondiale* (Paris 1958).

[J. G.] Sikes, [*Peter Abelard*] (Cambridge 1932).

E. Gilson, *Héloïse et Abelard*, 2. ed. (Paris 1948).

[A.] Börst, ['Abälard and Bernhard], *Historische Zeitschrift*, CLXXXVI (Munich 1958), pp. 497–526.

[J-M.] Dechanet, ['L'Amitié d'Abelard et de Guillaume de Saint Thierry'], *Revue d'histoire ecclesiastique*, XXXV (Louvain 1939).

D. Van den Eynde, 'Détails biographiques sur Pierre Abelard', *Antonianum*, XXXVIII (Rome 1963), pp. 220ff.

David Knowles, 'The Humanism of the Twelfth Century', repr. in *The Historian and Character* (Cambridge 1963), pp. 16–30.

[M. M.] McLaughlin, ['Abelard as Autobiographer: The Motives and Meaning of his "Story of Calamities"'], *Speculum*, XLII, 3 (Cambridge, Mass., 1967), pp. 463–88.

[J. R.] Martin, ['Pro Petro Abaelardo. Un plaidoyer de Robert de Melun contre Saint Bernard'], *Revue des Sciences Philosophiques et Theologiques*, XII (Paris 1923), pp. 308–33.

[A. R.] Motte, ['Une Fausse Accusation contre Abelard et Arnaud de Brescia'], *Revue des Sciences Philosophiques et Theologiques*, XXII (Paris 1933).

[J.] Riviére, ['Les "capitula" d'Abelard condamnés au concile de Sens'], *Recherches de Théologie Ancienne et Médiévale*, V (Louvain 1933), pp. 5–22.

[M-B. Carra de Vaux] Saint-Cyr, ['Disputatio catholicorum patrum adversus dogmata Petri Abaelardi'], *Revue des sciences philosophiques et theologiques*, XLVII (Paris 1963).

[R.] Oursel, [*La Dispute et la Grâce. Essai sur la Rédemption d'Abélard*] (Paris 1959).

A full account of the literature relating to Abelard can be found in *Ghellinck*, pp. 149ff., 278ff. Reference to more recent litera-

ture on Abelard can be found in *McLaughlin, art. cit.* References
to most of the literature relating to the dispute between Abelard
and Bernard can be found in *Borst*.

There is as yet no modern critical edition of all Abelard's
works. Recent editions of, and work on, Abelard's philosophical
and theological works are referred to above. For the rest,
Cousin's work, *Abaelardi Opera* (above), has been used. A new
edition and translation of the letters of Heloïse and Abelard is
in preparation by Professor R. W. Southern.

THE SYNOD OF SENS AND ITS AFTERMATH

(a) *The Synod*

The most important sources are:

Abelard: 'Letter to his Friends and Disciples' (see n. 17,
Ch. VII).

Bernard:

ep. 187 ('To the Bishops in France, Before the Synod'),
ep. 189 ('To the Pope, with a Report on the Synod'),
ep. 338 ('To Cardinal Haimeric, After the Synod'),
All in *Migne* CLXXXII.

Henry of Sens (and his fellow bishops): ep. 337 ('To the
Pope, on the Synod'), *Migne* CLXXXII.

Samson of Rheims (and his fellow bishops): ep. 191 ('To the
Pope, on the Synod'), *ibid.*

Geoffrey of Auxerre: in the 'Vita Bernardi', *Migne*
CLXXXV, cols 310–12.

Berengar of Poitiers: 'Apologeticus' (*apologia* for Abelard),
Abaelardi Opera II, pp. 771ff.

These last two are eye-witness accounts.

There are no official documents of the Synod.

(b) *The Aftermath*

Abelard: Letter and *Confessio fidei* to Heloïse, handed down
by Berengar in his *Apologeticus* (see above). *Abaelardi
Opera* I, pp. 68off.

*The Dialogue between a Philosopher, a Jew and a
Christian, ibid.* II, pp. 643–718.

Innocent II: Two letters of July 16, 1140, to Samson of Rheims, Henry of Sens, and Bernard, *Migne* CLXXIX.

Peter the Venerable: Letter to Innocent II concerning Abelard, *Abaelardi Opera* I, p. 709.

Two letters to Heloïse, *ibid.* I, pp. 710–14, 716.

Epitaph on Abelard, *ibid.* I, pp. 717ff.

Heloïse: Letter to Peter the Venerable, *ibid.* I, p. 715.

Berengar of Poitiers: *Apologeticus* (see above).

NOTES

CHAPTER 1

1. See H-J. Marrou, *Saint Augustin et la fin de la culture antique*, Bibliothèque des écoles française d'Athènes et de Rome, *fasc.* 145 (1938).
2. *Sidorova*, pp. 541–542.
3. See *Paré*, pp. 18ff. A corresponding development took place in Italy, where the study of law in particular flourished, with Bologna as its centre.
4. *Paré*, pp. 110ff.; *Grabmann*, II, pp. 13ff.
5. Translated from *Anselmi Opera*, I, pp. 100, 15ff.
6. See *Anselmi Opera*, II, pp. 6–7 ('Epistola de incarnatione verbi').
7. See *Grabmann*, I, pp. 285ff.
8. *ibid.* pp. 311ff.
9. *Seeberg*, pp. 163ff.
10. The following is based on *Kleineidam*, pp. 128–167.
11. The examples are taken from *Chenu*, pp. 343ff.
12. I owe the following characterization of the difference between monastic and scholastic theology to *Leclercq, Theologie Monastique*, pp. 7–28.
13. See *Klibansky's* commentaries on this.
14. The most important investigation of the epistolary literature of the period is that of *Ott, op. cit.*
15. See, in this connection, *Haskins*, ch. VI, 'Latin Poetry', pp. 153ff.

CHAPTER 2

1. For contemporary references to Abelard, *Ghellinck*, pp. 278ff. may be consulted. All necessary references may be found here.
2. *HC*, Ch. I.
3. See *Paré*, p. 106.
4. Roscelin left no philosophical writings, at least none that we know of. His viewpoint is known solely from the polemics against him of Anselm of Canterbury and Abelard. That Abelard was his pupil, however, appears to be proved by an existing letter from Roscelin to Abelard (see p. 75 below). Apart from

this, Abelard refers several times in his writings to Roscelin as
his teacher.

5. HC, Ch. II.
6. ibid.
7. ibid.
8. ibid.
9. See *Ghellinck*, pp. 133ff. and the references there given.
10. HC, Ch. III.
11. ibid.
12. ibid.
13. See also *Paré*, pp. 67ff.
14. HC, Ch. V.
15. *Paré*, pp. 57ff.
16. HC, Ch. V.

CHAPTER 3

1. HC, Ch. VI.
2. ibid.
3. *Abaelardi Opera* I, ep. 5, from Heloïse to Abelard.
4. ibid.
5. HC, Ch. VI.
6. *Abaelardi Opera* I, ep. 2, from Abelard to Heloïse.
7. ibid.
8. ibid.
9. HC, Ch. VI. See Peter the Venerable's letter of 1142 to Heloïse,
   Abaelardi Opera I, cols 710–714.
10. HC, Ch. VI.
11. ibid.
12. HC, Ch. VII.
13. ep. 5, loc. cit.
14. HC, Ch. V.
15. HC, Ch. VII.
16. ibid.
17. ibid.
18. For this see *Genest*, particularly pp. 80ff.
19. HC, Ch. VII.
20. ep. 2, loc. cit.
21. ibid.
22. ibid.
23. ibid.
24. ibid.
25. ep. 5, loc. cit.
26. HC, Ch. VIII.
27. *Abaelardi Opera* I, pp. 703–707, letter of canon Fulk of Deuil to
    Abelard. Fulk tries to persuade Abelard to abandon revenge.

The canon leads us to believe that it was Abelard's intention to conduct his own case before the papal curia. He warns him with a reference to the notorious avarice of the Roman curia. He will achieve nothing, but be robbed of everything – without justice being done to him!

28. HC, Ch. VIII.
29. ep. 2, loc. cit.
30. ibid.
31. Abaelardi Opera, I, ep. 4.
32. ep. 2, loc. cit.
33. ibid.
34. ep. 4, loc. cit.
35. ibid.
36. ibid.
37. ep. 5, loc. cit.
38. ibid.

CHAPTER 4

1. See, for example, Vacandard, I, pp. 178ff.
2. Abaelardi Opera, I, ep. 5. See HC, Ch. XIV. Fulk of Deuil already draws the obvious comparison, Abaelardi Opera, I, p. 705.
3. HC, Ch. IX.
4. Abaelardi Opera, II, pp. 150ff.
5. ibid. I, pp. 798–803. Roscelin's letter anticipates Abelard's move to the Paraclete. In his introductory comments Cousin assumes that it is this letter which has made Abelard write in anger to the Bishop of Paris asking him to arrange a disputation. This is, however, improbable, although it would, of course, have been rather satisfactory to be able in this way to bring the two letters into relation with one another. But on the other hand there is nothing in the letter to the Bishop of Paris to indicate that Abelard had already been sentenced at Soissons – quite the contrary. Moreover, an application to the Bishop of Paris would have been quite absurd if it had originated from the Paraclete, whereas it would be quite natural from St Denis. We must, therefore, take into account an attack, unknown to us, on Abelard by Roscelin.
6. This is apparent not only from Abelard's own account in HC, Chs. IX–X; it is expressly confirmed by Otto of Freising, Bk I, Ch. XLVII – without his being given the opportunity to reply.
7. HC, Ch. X.
8. Abaelardi Opera, I, pp. 681ff.
9. ibid. I, pp. 708ff.

CHAPTER 5

1. Some of the philosophical writings are published in *Geyer, Beiträge*. A number of glossaries on Aristotle, Porphyry and Boëthius have been published by M. *dal Pra* (Milan 1954), and the *Dialectica* by L. M. *de Rjik*. Useful information on Abelard's logic is given in *Geyer's* conclusion and de Rjik's introduction.

2. See *Geyer, Beiträge*, p. 630.

3. The example is taken from *Gilson*.

4. See also the concluding comments in *Geyer, Beiträge*, and also *Ueberweg*, pp. 216ff.

5. *HC*, Ch. III.

6. *Abaelardi Opera*, II, pp. 67, 73, *Theologia* II. In contrast to the philosophical works, there are as yet, with one exception, no theological works in a satisfactory critical edition. The exception is Ostlender, *Theologia Summi Boni*, which is identical with the book condemned by the Synod of Soissons in 1121. Most of the remaining theological works may be found in *Abaelardi Opera*. The methodical programme work *Sic et Non*, not included in that work, may be found in *Migne CLXXVIII*.

7. See below n. 29.

8. *Abaelardi Opera*, II, p. 3, *Theologia* I.

9. *ibid.* II, pp. 72ff., *Theologia* II.

10. A constantly repeated theme with Abelard. See, for example, *Theologia* II (*Abaelardi Opera*, II, pp. 3, 93, 97) and 'Letter to an Anti-dialectician' (*ibid.* I, pp. 695ff.).

11. See, for example, *HC*, Ch. III.

12. See, for example, 'Letter to an Anti-dialectician' (n. 10 above) where Abelard, by way of introduction, uses the story of the fox and the sour grapes (which for Abelard, however, are cherries!) against the opponents of dialectic.

13. *HC*, Ch. IX.

14. *Anselmi Opera*, II, pp. 39ff. Letter to Pope Urban II together with the presentation of the treatise *Cur Deus homo*.

15. *Abaelardi Opera*, II, pp. 9-10, *Theologia* I: 'The faith is indeed catholic, that is to say universal, which is so necessary for all that nobody can be saved without it.'

16. *ibid.* II, p. 83, *Theologia* II.

17. *HC*, Ch. IX.

18. *Abaelardi Opera*, II, p. 67, *Theologia* II.

19. *ibid.* II, p. 72, *Theologia* II.

20. *ibid.* II, pp. 28ff., *Theologia* I.

21. See the informative table, in *Abaelardi Opera*, II, of those *auctores* cited by Abelard.

22. See *Sikes*, p. 66 and *Chenu*, pp. 32ff., 121ff.

23. In the *Dialectica* he rejects the identification of the Holy Ghost with *anima mundi* (Rjik, pp. 558ff.). For the growing scepticism towards the philosophers' general concept of God see *Cottiaux*, pp. 280ff.

24. The dating problems are difficult – see *Cottiaux's* careful research (*op. cit.*, pp. 280ff.). The sequence, however, is quite certain: *Theologia Summi Boni – Theologia Christiana – Theologia*. The last-named, following an erroneous manuscript note, is often referred to as *Introductio ad Theologiam*. For the transmission of manuscripts and the conclusions to be drawn from them as to the different versions of Abelard's works see *Ostlender, Theologia Scholarium*, pp. 262–81.

25. See *Ghellinck*, pp. 83, 91ff; *Cottiaux*, p. 270.

26. *Abaelardi Opera*, II, p. 12, *Theologia* I.

27. *ibid.* II, p. 93, *Theologia* II.

28. *ibid.* II, p. 447, *Theologia Christiana* III.

29. *ibid.* II, pp. 88ff., *Theologia* II.

30. *ibid.* II, p. 67, *Theologia* II.

31. *ibid.* II, p. 79, *Theologia* II.

32. *ibid.* II, pp. 12ff., *Theologia* I.

33. *ibid.* II, pp. 97–102, *Theologia* II.

34. *ibid.* II, pp. 100–102, *Theologia* II.

35. See *Ostlender, Theologia Summi Boni*, p. 94.

36. *Sikes*, p. 149.

37. *Abaelardi Opera*, II, p. 462, *Theologia Christiana* III.

38. *ibid.* II, pp. 115–119, *Theologia* III.

39. *ibid.* II, pp. 120–132, *Theologia* III.

40. *ibid.* II, pp. 142–145, *Theologia* III.

41. The supposition, frequently repeated in older literature, that part of the *Theologia* has been lost, can now be rejected on the basis of *Ostlender's* work on the manuscripts (see n. 24 above).

42. *Abaelardi Opera*, II, pp. 206–207, 'Commentary on the Epistle to the Romans'.

43. *ibid.* II, p. 207.

44. *ibid.*, p. 596, Éthica.

45. *ibid.* II, p. 599.

46. *ibid.* II, pp. 600ff.

47. *ibid.* II, pp. 602ff.

48. *ibid.* II, pp. 614ff.

49. *ibid.* II, pp. 615ff.

50. *ibid.* II, p. 618.

CHAPTER 6

As the information given in this chapter concerning Bernard's life and activities may be easily found in any biography, and as the account of his thought is derived entirely from existing literature, particularly Gilson, *Mystical Theology*, this chapter is not provided with consecutive notes.

CHAPTER 7

1. In support of the theory that the *Theologia* was written during Abelard's period at the Paraclete it has been pointed out that the towns mentioned are located around the Paraclete, and that the names of the four masters, in Abelard's opinion heretics, given in Book II also fit in geographically with this location. See *Cottiaux*, p. 257.
2. *Metalogicon*, Bk II, Ch. 10.
3. *William of St Thierry*, cols 249–282.
4. *Migne CLXXXII*, ep. 326.
5. See *Klibansky*, p. 11.
6. HC, Ch. XII.
7. Abelard mocks Norbert and his 'fellow apostle' Farsitus in a malicious manner in a sermon – *Abaelardi Opera*, I, p. 590, Sermon XXXIII.
8. *Borst* seeks, in a rather artificial manner, to prove that the two 'apostles' were Norbert and Farsitus (n. 7 above), whom he wishes to identify with Norbert's successor as abbot-general, Hugh of Fosse. However, it is not easy to see why, in that case, Abelard should refer to, and distinguish between, these two Premonstratensians as the leaders of regular canons and monks. See *Borst*, pp. 501ff.
9. *Migne CLXXXII*, col. 1031, Bernard, *De Baptismo*.
10. *Abaelardi Opera*, II, pp. 618ff. This letter to Bernard begins with a few words about Heloïse and the nuns having received Bernard not as a man, but as an angel. Abelard also speaks of the affection which Bernard has for him. Then, however, he comes to the point, and after a long explanation ends by saying that he is standing firm on his position. In fact, no useful conclusion as to their relationship can be arrived at on the basis of this letter.
11. See *Borst*, p. 504.
12. *Chronicum Mauriniacense*, pp. 40ff.
13. *Dechanet*, pp. 761–774.
14. *Migne CLXXXII*, ep. 326.

15. The work referred to here is unknown to us. From Ostlender's comparison of the known works of Abelard's disciples, however, it is clear that besides the *Theologia* they have another source in common. There is scarcely any doubt that this is the book that Bernard refers to as *Liber Sententiarum*. See *Ostlender Sentenzenbücher*, pp. 208–252.

16. Otto of Freising, a Cistercian, says, however, of Bernard, in connection with the Abelard matter in particular, that he was always very willing to believe denunciations of heresy. *Otto of Freising*, Bk I, Ch. XLVII.

17. *Migne* CLXXXII, ep. 327.

18. According to Geoffrey of Auxerre, Bernard's biographer, Abelard is said to have promised in repentance to correct his teaching, but prompted by evil advisors to have abandoned this undertaking after Bernard had left. Geoffrey also ascribes a part in his altered decision to Abelard's misplaced confidence in his own skill in debate. See *Migne* CLXXXV, col. 311, *Vita Prima Bernardi*, Bk III, Ch. V, 14.

A letter to the pope from the archbishop of Sens and his suffragans (a report of the Synod of Sens 1140) says that Bernard initially cautioned Abelard secretly, and then, following the advice of the Gospel, in the presence of two or three witnesses. This he was supposed to have done in all friendliness – *amicabiliter satis et familiariter. Migne* CLXXXII, ep. 337.

A letter only recently published (*Leclercq, Études*, pp. 104ff.; *Klibansky, art. cit.*) from Abelard to his friends, written immediately before the synod, says that until then Bernard had professed to be a friend, indeed a very firm friend – *amicissimus*. This appears to confirm that the discussions between Abelard and Bernard took place in a friendly atmosphere. It is against this background that Abelard considered Bernard's action to be an act of treachery.

19. See Geoffrey of Auxerre, n. 18 above.

20. See Borst, pp. 508ff.

21. *Klibansky*, pp. 6ff. See n. 18 above.

22. *Migne* CLXXXII, cols. 853ff., 'De Conversione ad Clericos'. See also the bishops' report to the pope on the Synod of Sens (n. 18 above), which refers to Bernard's action towards Abelard's pupils. After mentioning the meetings between Abelard and Bernard it continues – 'He [Bernard] also requested of several of the students that they should surrender and reject the books, which were full of poison, and that they should abstain from a teaching which was harmful to the Catholic faith.'

This praiseworthy effort on the part of the pious abbot was certainly well suited to emphasize his merits to the pope, but not to strengthen his credit with Abelard!

23. See *Ostlender, Theologia Scholarium*, pp. 272ff., and n. 24, Ch. V

above. The fourth version is identical with the printed text. According to *Ostlender, op. cit.* William and Bernard have both used the third version.

24. *Borst* (p. 510, n. 3) has objected to the interpretation of ep. 330 as a draft of ep. 189. He points out that Abelard is compared to a dragon in both places. In ep. 330, however, the dragon is lying in wait, whereas in ep. 189 it has clearly appeared. This, however, does not prove that two separate letters are involved. Ep. 330 might be considered as a draft, dating from before Sens, and ep. 189 as the final, edited and despatched version – Borst refers to other instances of drafting and subsequent correction. It is doubtful, too, whether, as Borst believes, ep. 330 is an actual letter from the period before the Synod of Sens, since it contains some lines which are incomprehensible if they were written at that time. After a short description of Abelard's heresy, ep. 330 reads as follows:

'But in all this he [Abelard] boasts that he has opened the sources of knowledge to the cardinals and priests of the Curia, that he has placed his books and sentences in the hands and hearts of the Romans, and in defence of his error he looks to those by whom he ought to be judged, and condemned. In what spirit, with what conscience, do you seek refuge with the defender of the Faith, you persecutor of the Faith? How can you be so brazen, show such effrontery, in paying such attention to the friend of the Bridegroom [the Pope], you ravisher of the Bride [the Church]? If only the care of my brethren did not detain me, my bodily weakness prevent me! How I desire to see the friend of the Bridegroom fighting on the Bride's behalf in the absence of the Bridegroom!'

Then follows a request to the pope to defend the Bride of Christ. This section appears to me to be incomprehensible if it does not imply a knowledge of Abelard's appeal to Rome at the Synod of Sens. It cannot be objected that the letter does not expressly refer to this appeal: letters were being despatched, at the same time, by the bishops to the pope with an official report on the progress of the Synod. Bernard's ardent wish to see the pope defend the Church and to remain firm towards the heretic, which official duties and bad health prevented he himself from doing, only makes sense if it was foreseen that Abelard would soon arrive at Rome. Consequently, *Borst's* interpretation must be rejected. Ep. 330 is only a draft, and from the period *after* Sens.

25. This refers to ep. 192 (to Cardinal Guy of Castello), 193 (Cardinal Ivo), 331 (Cardinal Stephen), 332 (Cardinal G –) and perhaps 336 (an abbot). Letter 338 (to Cardinal Haimeric, the papal

Chancellor) has the same general character, but certain features clearly foreshadow the events at Sens. It can therefore be assumed that the letter was drafted before the Synod, but not despatched until afterwards.

26. This list is mentioned in ep. 190 (*Migne* CLXXXII, col. 1072), the 'Treatise on the Errors of Abelard', and also in Abelard's letter to his friends (see n. 18 above), but is not known to us. It has recently been announced, however, that the list can be found in more than twenty-five manuscripts of Bernard's letters. See *Leclercq, Etudes,* pp. 101ff.

27. *Migne* CLXXXII, ep. 188. In this Bernard mentions 'the book that he, Abelard, calls the *Theologia*', and later refers to 'that other book which they call the Book of the Sentences and also the one entitled *Know Thyself*'. However, he makes a distinction here between 'that he calls' and 'which they call'. Is this a claim that the *Book of Sentences* is of the same kind as the other two mentioned?

    Abelard later denied that he had ever written a book called the *Book of Sentences.*

    Leclercq, Etudes, p. 102, notes that Bernard's list of Abelard's errors, which follows ep. 190, has the following concluding comment:

    'Haec capitula partim in libro Theologiae, partim in libro Sententiarum magistri Petri, partim in libro cuius titulus Scito teipsum reperta sunt.'

28. *Klibansky,* p. 19.
29. *Migne* CLXXXII, ep. 193.
30. ibid. ep. 183, 332.
31. ibid. ep. 332.
32. ibid. ep. 193.
33. ibid. ep. 332.
34. ibid. ep. 193, 331.
35. ibid. ep. 193.
36. ibid. ep. 331.
37. ibid. ep. 193.
38. ibid.
39. ibid. ep. 331.
40. ibid. ep. 336.
41. ibid. ep. 190, *Treatise on the Errors of Abelard.*
42. ibid. cols 1055, 1059 (the second Aristotle), 1066.
43. ibid. cols 1062ff.
44. This question will be examined later.
45. *Migne* CLXXXII, cols 1070ff.
46. *Ostlender, Theologia Scholarium* (see n. 24, Ch. V above), has dealt briefly with these alterations. I hope to be able to publish a more detailed investigation later.

CHAPTER 8

1. See n. 18, Ch. VII.
2. See Bernard's tract to the pope, *Migne CLXXXII*, col. 1061.
3. The two editors of the letter do not agree on who appealed to the archbishop to ask him to summon Bernard. *Leclercq, Etudes,* believes it was the friends; *Klibansky,* on the other hand, has hitherto thought that it was Abelard himself. It depends on whether one reads *iuxta petitionem vestram* or *nostram,* according to your request – according to our request (that is, Abelard's). To me, it does not appear to be particularly important. If Abelard's friends made the application they probably did so with Abelard's approval. Perhaps, however, *Klibansky's* reading is the more likely: both Bernard and the archbishop in their letters to the pope (ep. 189, 337) made Abelard the person responsible.
4. This list, now rediscovered (see n. 26, Ch. VII), is missing completely from manuscripts deriving from Clairvaux. *Leclercq, Etudes,* suggests that this may be because it was wished to protect Bernard's reputation, later assailed by Abelard's *Apologia.* At all events this disappearance is interesting, and it seems that someone's conscience was not very clear.
5. *Migne CLXXXII,* ep. 182.
6. See *ibid.* ep. 189.
7. In the letter, Bernard gives two parallel reasons for his refusal. He refused first because he could only be regarded as a child in a disputation such as this, whereas Abelard had been trained as a dialectician for such disputations since his earliest youth, and secondly because he considered it unworthy to make faith, which rests on certain and immovable truth, the subject of disputation. Bernard does not seem to see that the latter makes the first reason redundant. Why does he adduce it? Because it is the true reason for his refusal, whereas the other is to confirm to himself that he *ought* not to do what he *dares* not do – a text-book example of the psychological mechanism that we call *rationalization.*
8. *Migne CLXXXII,* ep. 189. In this, Bernard probably alludes to the letter from Abelard referred to. As that letter clearly suggests a knowledge of Bernard's tract to the pope, we can be certain that Abelard's appeal at Seur was preceded by Bernard's action in Rome.
9. See *ibid.* ep. 189, 337 (the Archbishop of Sens' report to the pope).
10. *ibid.* ep. 187.
11. It is doubtful whether anything, apart from incompatibility with

Bernard, united Abelard and Arnold. Otto of Freising, it is true, says that Arnold had been Abelard's disciple, but it is probable that he was only in France once, in 1139–40. This is clearly attested by John of Salisbury, who was himself in Paris at the time. For further details see *Motte*, pp. 27–46.

12. See *Migne* CLXXXII, ep. 189.
13. *Abaelardi Opera*, II, p. 772, the *Apologeticus* of Berengar of Poitiers.
14. *Migne* CLXXXII, ep. 189, 338. Apart from Berengar the negotiations preceding the Synod are attested by the Archbishop of Sens, ep. 337.
15. *Abaelardi Opera*, II, pp. 772ff.
16. *Vacandard*, II, p. 147.
17. Geoffrey of Auxerre maintains that Abelard appealed in a moment of distraction in order to gain time (*Migne* CLXXXV, col. 311). In ep. 189 (*Migne* CLXXXII), Bernard maintains that Abelard interrupted the reading out of the *capitula* and refused to listen to them, but here his evidence is in conflict with that of Geoffrey of Auxerre and of the Archbishop of Sens (ep. 337).
18. See Geoffrey of Auxerre, *loc. cit.*, and the letters of the Archbishops of Sens and Rheims to the pope, *Migne* CLXXXII, ep. 337, 191.
19. *Abaelardi Opera*, II, p. 775.
20. See Bernard's letter to the pope, *Migne* CLXXXII, ep. 189.
21. The quotation reads: '*Nam tua res agitur, paries cum proximus ardet.*' See Geoffrey of Auxerre, *Migne* CLXXXV, col. 312.
22. An interesting description of this matter, of such little credit to Bernard, is given in *Poole*, pp. 156ff. The cardinals present at the Synod of Rheims refused to agree to a secret meeting before the Synod, pointing out that this was the same method which Bernard had employed at Sens against Abelard. The abbot's methods were now known, and he was, indeed, completely unsuccessful in repeating against Gilbert what he had been lucky enough to succeed in against Abelard.
23. *Migne* CLXXXII, ep. 191 (Letter of the Province of Rheims).
24. *ibid.* ep. 337.
25. *ibid.* ep. 189.
26. *ibid.* ep. 338.
27. Besides ep. 338, ep. 333, 334 and 335, to different cardinals, are relevant.
28. The long-standing disagreement among students of Abelard about the number and content of the *capitula* may be considered to have been resolved by *Rivière*.
29. *Abaelardi Opera*, II, pp. 719–723.
30. *Ruf-Grabmann*.
31. In *Confessio fidei* (*Abaelardi Opera*, II, p. 772), Abelard quotes Bernard as follows: 'These "capitula" are in part found in the

Book of Theology, in part in master Peter's *Book of Sentences*, and in part in the book of which the title is *Know Thyself.*' These very words do in fact follow Bernard's list of *capitula*, and there is, consequently, good reason to assume that Abelard had this before him. See *Leclercq*, *Etudes*, pp. 101ff., and n. 26, Ch. VII above.

32. See *Borst*, p. 514.
33. *William of St Thierry*, cols 257, 259; Bernard, *Migne* CLXXXII, cols 1056, 1059ff.
34. See the text of the *Apologia* (*Ruf-Grabmann*, pp. 10ff.). In *Confessio fidei* Abelard says that he detests the first sentence which he considers not only heretical but satanic (*Abaelardi Opera*, II, p. 720).
35. The fragment breaks off just as Abelard begins the refutation of the second sentence: 'That the Holy Ghost is not of (*ex*) the substance of the Father'. Here also there is a misunderstanding, as is apparent from William's and Bernard's attacks (*Migne* CLXXX, cols 262ff.; CLXXXII, cols 1056ff.) and Abelard's reply in the fourth and fifth versions of the *Theologia*.

It would lead us too far to go into the question in more detail here. Suffice it to say that Abelard had no thought of denying that the three Persons of the Trinity are of the same, indeed of one, substance. The expression criticized serves to distinguish the Son from the Holy Spirit, and is explained in more detail by considerations of linguistic logic. It is understandable that Abelard's speculations on the *anima mundi* concept should give rise to criticism, but when this leads to the Holy Ghost *being* the World Soul (see *William of Thierry*, cols 265ff., and the *capitula*) this again is a misunderstanding. It is, of course, not quite the same to say, as Abelard does, that Plato in the concept of an *anima mundi* faintly perceives the Holy Ghost, and that the Holy Ghost is the World Soul. Abelard never said the latter, and he gave up the former.

36. There is more substance in the fifth sentence: 'That neither God, nor man, nor the person who is Christ is the third person of the Trinity'. It was William of Thierry who drew attention to this problem (cols 277ff.). It is quite clear that Abelard's theory of the immutability of God presents difficulties for him when he has to explain that Christ has become man. How can it be said, he asks in the third book of the *Theologia*, that the Word became flesh or God became man, for the Word, since it was God before the Incarnation, is Spirit, while man is physical? His answer to this is that God in the proper sense (*proprie*) cannot be said to be man or flesh, otherwise man also, conversely, could be said to be God: this cannot be said of anything created, since everything that is created has a beginning. The immutability of God must be strictly insisted upon (*Abaelardi Opera*,

II, pp. 136ff.). We do not find here the claim that William of St Thierry complains about, but it cannot be denied that the content of this complaint is the consequence of what is adduced. The Person Who is Christ means, after all, the Incarnate: God and Man. It would be difficult for Abelard to say of Him that He is the third Person of the Trinity. This can only be said of the Word, which, in its unity with human nature, is also immutably preserved.

It may be said, then, that it is difficult for Abelard to see Christ as a man. In the Incarnation, also, it is God's eternal wisdom and Word which preoccupy him. In this he is vastly different from William of St Thierry and Bernard whose thoughts on humility concentrate upon Jesus the Man in His historical form. Consequently they are intent upon the suffering of the God-man as a model of humility, while Abelard sees in the sufferings of Christ primarily the revelation of God's love. The difference is clear enough and had to lead, of course, to the rejection of Abelard by Bernard and William.

37. *William of Thierry*, cols 281ff.
38. 'Commentary on the Roman Letter' (*Abaelardi Opera*, II, p. 238); *Ethica* (ibid. II, p. 616).
39. 'Commentary on the Roman Letter' (*ibid.* II, p. 243).
40. *Anselmi Opera*, I, cols 259ff., (*De casu diaboli*, Ch. XVI).
41. 'Commentary on the Roman Letter' (*Abaelardi Opera*, II, p. 246).
42. *William of St Thierry*, col. 282.
43. See above pp. 116ff.
44. Migne CLXXXII, ep. 332, states that Abelard had put '*aquas furtivas et panes absconditos*' before his domestics (*domesticos*). In *Confessio fidei* (*Abaelardi Opera*, II, p. 720) Abelard claimed that his teaching had never contained '*aquas furtivas vel panem absconditum*'. These are both references to the *Vulgate* (Proverbs IX, 17), where the verse reads: '*Aquae furtivae dulciores sunt, et panis absconditus suavior*' (Stolen waters are sweet, and bread eaten in secret is pleasant).

CHAPTER 9

1. *Migne* CLXXIX, cols 515–517.
2. In a letter to a cardinal, see *Abaelardi Opera*, I, p. 70.
3. See Borst, p. 523.
4. *Migne* CLXXXII, ep. 337.
5. Letter to Innocent II (see above); see letter to Heloïse, *Abaelardi Opera*, I, p. 713 (penultimate line).
6. *Abaelardi Opera*, II, p. 645.
7. *ibid.* I, cols 710–714.

8. ibid.
9. See ibid. I, col. 710.
10. Abaelardi Opera, I, p. 715.
11. ibid. I, pp. 716ff. Strangely enough, Astrolabius is not mentioned at all in the correspondence between Abelard and Heloïse. Evidence of Abelard's preoccupation with his son can be found in a long didactic poem to him, ibid. I, pp. 340ff.
12. ibid. I, ep. 4.
13. Berengar of Poitiers, Apologeticus, Abaelardi Opera, II, pp. 771ff.
14. ibid.
15. Abaelardi Opera, II, p. 778.
16. ibid. II, pp. 786ff.
17. The dispute also had a sequel on the opposing side. Abelard's Apologia, which was of course directed at Bernard, was countered by an anonymous person who wrote at the request of the Archbishop of Rouen. It is to be found, erroneously, among William of St Thierry's works (cols 283ff.).

    Saint-Cyr is of the opinion that the anonymous disputatio was written by Thomas, Abbot of Morigny, as an answer to Abelard's great Apologia.

    Oursel argues that the anonymous disputatio and Abelard's Apologia must have been written before the Council at Sens (see in particular 'Note critique', pp. 89ff.). It appears, however, that Oursel does not know the fragment of the Apologia published by Ruf-Grabmann, and therefore his conclusions are arrived at on an insufficient basis. The fragment indisputably proves that the nineteen propositions that were condemned at Sens are axiomatic for Abelard's Apologia.
18. See Martin.
19. See the comments in Ruf-Grabmann, pp. 29ff.
20. Abaelardi Opera, I, col. 717.
21. See Poole, pp. 171ff.
22. See Ostlender, Sentenzenbücher (see n. 14, Ch. I). For further references see Ghellinck, p. 158, n. 2.
23. See William of St Thierry's treatise against William of Conches (Migne CLXXX, cols 333-340).
24. See Ghellinck, p. 153, ns. 1, 3. Walter of St Victor, 'Contra quatuor Labyrinthos Franciae' (Migne CXCIX, cols 1127-1172).
25. See John of Cornwall (the Lombard's disciple), Eulogium, Ch. III (Migne CXCIX, cols 1052ff.).
26. See Ghellinck, pp. 201ff.

Index

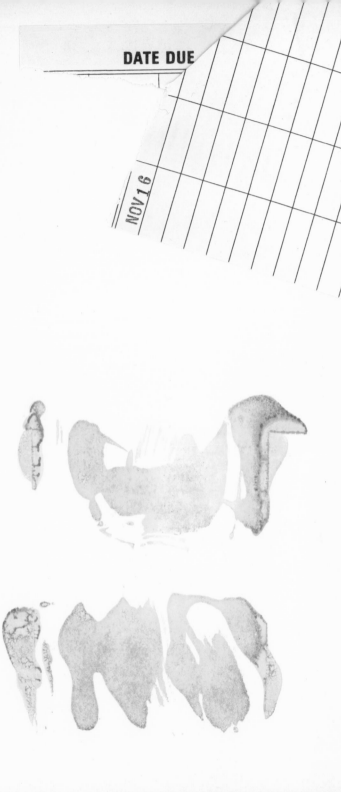